Jafar Panahi: Interviews

Conversations with Filmmakers Series
Gerald Peary, General Editor

Jafar Panahi
INTERVIEWS

Edited by Drew Todd

Ehsan Khoshbakht (London), Assistant Editor

University Press of Mississippi / Jackson

The University Press of Mississippi is the scholarly publishing agency of
the Mississippi Institutions of Higher Learning: Alcorn State University,
Delta State University, Jackson State University, Mississippi State University,
Mississippi University for Women, Mississippi Valley State University,
University of Mississippi, and University of Southern Mississippi.

www.upress.state.ms.us

The University Press of Mississippi is a member of the Association of University Presses.

Publication of this work was made possible in part by a generous donation from
the College of Humanities and the Arts at San José State University.

First printing 2019

∞

Library of Congress Cataloging-in-Publication Data

Names: Panahi, Jafar, interviewee. | Todd, Drew, 1970– editor.
Title: Jafar Panahi: interviews / edited by Drew Todd.
Description: Jackson: University Press of Mississippi, [2019] | Series:
   Conversations with Filmmakers Series | Includes bibliographical references
   and index. |
Identifiers: LCCN 2019004379 (print) | LCCN 2019013244 (ebook) | ISBN
   9781496823212 (epub single) | ISBN 9781496823229 (epub institutional) |
   ISBN 9781496823236 (pdf single) | ISBN 9781496823243 (pdf institutional)
   | ISBN 9781496823199 (cloth) | ISBN 9781496823205 (pbk.)
Subjects: LCSH: Panahi, Jafar. | Motion picture producers and
   directors—Iran—Interviews. | LCGFT: Interviews.
Classification: LCC PN1998.3.P34522 (ebook) | LCC PN1998.3.P34522 A5 2019
   (print) | DDC 791.4302/33092 [B]—dc23 LC record available at https://lccn.loc.gov/2019004379

British Library Cataloging-in-Publication Data available

Contents

Introduction

A few years after its release, I started teaching *The Circle* (2000) in an undergraduate survey of international cinema. I hoped to find some scholarship in English that would help my students analyze this complicated, subtle Iranian film. The only sources that offered both context and analysis were interviews with the director himself. In them, Jafar Panahi spoke eloquently of the path he took to becoming a filmmaker and of how he transitioned from making movies about children to those about adults. As I taught his works made after *The Circle*—*Crimson Gold* (2003), *Offside* (2006), and then *This is Not a Film* (2011)—I continued assigning his interviews. (In my opinion, that quartet of successive films is as strong as you'll find in any filmmaker's oeuvre.) The more I read, the more I understood Panahi's intentions as a filmmaker.

Even after Panahi's arrest by Iranian authorities in 2010, when he was banned for twenty years from making movies and giving interviews, he has persisted in speaking out—through an array of open letters and public statements, through his illicit films (he has made four since his 2010 arrest) and clandestine interviews (including one given exclusively for this publication). This collection of his words and thoughts frames Panahi's body of work and also his struggles as an Iranian filmmaker. If the objective of Iran's government has been to silence Jafar Panahi, then may this collection project his voice far and wide.

Born in 1960 in Iran's northwestern province of East Azerbaijan, Jafar Panahi's boyhood occurred during a significant but precarious period in Iran's film history. The Iranian New Wave emerged under the shadow of the Shah in the late 1960s and early 1970s, embracing a new kind of cinematic realism. Filmmakers such as Dariush Mehrjui (*The Cow*, 1969) and Bahram Beyzaie (*Downpour*, 1972)—both of whom Panahi cites as influences in a 1995 *Film Monthly* interview—did not shy away from political content and formal experimentation. A young Abbas Kiarostami started his film career in the same period with the highly influential short *The Bread and Alley* (1970). Kiarostami would inspire a generation of Iranian filmmakers, none more so than Panahi.

In 1979, the Iranian Revolution ushered in a Shia Muslim theocracy, thus putting an end to 2,500 continuous years of Persian monarchy. With regime change, Iran's first wave came to a halt. The Islamic revolutionaries perceived movies as a vestige of Western capitalism and thus inherently decadent and corrupting. (In the summer of 1978, Cinema Rex movie theater in Abadan, Iran had been burned to the ground by religious-based arsonists, killing nearly 500 patrons locked inside.) Once in power, the new Islamist regime nationalized most media and outlawed exhibition of Hollywood and Western cinema. Just as Panahi was gravitating toward a career in film, the Islamic Republic of Iran made clear that cinema would thereafter be contested and highly censored (if not, with controversial subjects, outright banned).

Even before the revolution, cinema was a source of contention for Panahi. As he discusses in his interview with Liza Béar, the local movie theater was off limits to him when he was a boy; he went anyway, against his father's strict orders, determined to see what he had been told "was not good for me." When the Iran-Iraq War commenced shortly after the revolution, he was assigned to the army's cinematography unit and then captured by Kurdish rebels, who held him captive for two months. When making short documentaries for Iranian TV in the late 1980s, he went undercover to film dangerous and illegal rituals. *The Wounded Heads* (1988), about the mourning practice of head slashing in Northern Iran, was banned for several years, presaging his future as one of Iran's most controversial and polarizing directors.

As the catastrophic Iran–Iraq War came to an end in the late 1980s, Iran's commercial film industry was resurrected. In spite of draconian state regulations and censorship, the Second Wave thrived in the following decades, applauded by critics and enjoying festival and box office success the world over. Abbas Kiarostami and Mohsen Makhmalbaf became the Second Wave's most important directors. Meanwhile, Panahi was transitioning from shorts to features, which he did under the tutelage of Kiarostami, who hired him as assistant director of *Through the Olive Trees* (1994). In several interviews in this volume, Panahi details Kiarostami's methods, many of which became his own as a filmmaker: the synthesis of documentary and fiction; a preference for child characters and nonprofessional actors; the privileging of image over script and plot; the obsessive search for faces, locations, and shots; the hands-on director as *auteur* who comes up with story ideas, finds actors and locations, and even edits his own films; and an unorthodox "scripting" that is open-ended. (The interviews also articulate important distinctions between Panahi and his mentor.)

As production on *Through the Olive Trees* wrapped up, Kiarostami was solicited to write (or to spontaneously orate, as the case may be) the screenplay that would become Panahi's debut picture, *The White Balloon* (1995). (Nearly a decade later Kiarostami also "scripted" Panahi's underappreciated *Crimson Gold*.) *The White Balloon* was received warmly in Iran and remains his most viewed film in his own country. For a spell, Iranian national TV would broadcast it every year around *Nowruz* (Persian New Year). Panahi's debut did well abroad, too, winning the Caméra d'Or at Cannes for the best first feature. In the US, it became at its release the highest-grossing Iranian film.

In his sophomore production, *The Mirror* (1997), Panahi again focused on a child as protagonist. It is well known that Iranian filmmakers have faced less censorial oversight when making movies about children, but Panahi indicates in his interviews that it was filmic influences that most inspired him: Kiarostami's short *The Bread and Alley*, about a little boy and a loaf of bread, and Vittorio De Sica's *Bicycle Thieves* (1948), about a father and his son. Panahi is most often labeled a neorealist, and not just because he cites *Bicycle Thieves* as a primary influence. His use of nonprofessional actors, preference for shooting on-location and in sequence, incorporation of real-time events, and his movies' lack of a score and special effects, all reinforce the label. Yet in *The Mirror*, Panahi also pushed the boundaries of realist narrative, doing away with the conventional divide between movie and audience, actor and character. Midway through the picture, Mina (Mina Mohammad Khani), playing a character trying to get home, decides she's done acting. She announces into the camera that she herself wants to go home (hence the title), as the film crew tries to convince her to keep making the movie and to stay in character. And all of this is scripted.

In his next three films, Panahi shifted attention away from children and toward controversial social topics, as they play out on the streets of Tehran. In *The Circle* and *Offside* he spotlights gender apartheid; in *Crimson Gold*, class conflict and economic disparity. In each case Panahi exposes limited social mobility in a country that forbids house parties and criminalizes women who have children out of wedlock or who try to attend sporting events. While continuing to experiment with cinematic narrative, Panahi boldly documented how social limitations oppress and divide Iranians.

Not surprisingly, Iran's Ministry of Culture and Islamic Guidance banned *The Circle* and *Crimson Gold*—the director refused to re-edit them—and restricted the distribution of *Offside*. According to his interviews and open letters, Panahi is deeply disappointed that Iranian audiences have not been able to see his movies at their local theaters. However, these three films were distributed widely abroad, drawing critical praise and awards, including top prizes at three of the most respected international film festivals: Venice, Cannes, and Berlin.

It was in this period that Panahi began to have serious encounters with the authorities, both in and out of Iran. He was twice detained by foreign customs agencies in transit between festivals. In one of several open letters included here, Panahi details his detainment at New York's John F. Kennedy Airport, where he was chained to a bench overnight. In 2009, Iran's Ministry of Intelligence arrested and then released him. On March 1, 2010, he was arrested again and this time imprisoned. Mainly due to international pressure—from governments, humanitarian agencies, and filmmakers—he was out on bail in three months. Later that year he was tried and convicted of anti-government propaganda and sentenced to six years in prison. Fortunately Iran's government has so far not enforced the prison sentence, but in effect is the twenty-year ban on Panahi leaving the country, writing and making movies, and giving interviews.

In the midst of court proceedings and his filmmaking ban, Panahi returned to his earliest roots as a nonfiction filmmaker and made an illegal documentary. Shot in Panahi's own flat with a digital camcorder and an iPhone, *This is Not a Film* chronicles his daily life awaiting the outcome of his appeal and imagining (and sometimes enacting) how he would realize his cinematic vision if only he were allowed. Panahi had long documented social struggles and situations in his native country; here he chronicles his own, defiantly turning the camera on himself. He has since made three more movies illegally, appearing as Jafar Panahi in all of them: *Closed Curtain* (2013), *Taxi* (2015), and, the latest, *3 Faces* (2018), with its world premiere at Cannes.

One consequence of producing films under such constraints has been to render Panahi's modernist aesthetic more visible. Actually, it's been there all along—or at least since *The Mirror*—combining self-reflexivity with a clear penchant for experimentation. He is quick to renounce commercialism, the star system, and leading the audience. In his interview with Ahmad Talebinejad, he recounts coming down with a fever in response to accepting commercial work early in his career. In his defense before an Iranian court, Panahi sounded like a surrealist when he queried, "Should artists be criminalized for the inner workings of their minds?" As he explains in an interview with Richard Porton, though the neorealists are prominent among his influences, so are Buñuel, Godard, and New Wave cinema, none more so than Iran's. An important feature of the Iranian New Wave is a modernist treatment of realism, in which formal experimentation nuances and heightens cinematic verisimilitude. This legacy clearly informs Panahi's filmmaking.

The topic of politics comes up repeatedly in his interviews, and Panahi's ambivalence on this point may surprise some. There are political ideas in his cinema, as he admits when pressed by Stephen Teo and David Walsh in their respective interviews, but I think his rejection of the "political" label may be lost in translation. For Panahi, the word "politics" means partisanship and favoring one party or government over another. When distinguishing between people and government, society and state, he favors the former in every instance. His condemnation of oppression and injustice does not discriminate against nations or governments.

His open letters, in which he speaks out against American as well as Iranian injustices, confirm as much. In his interview about *The Circle* with David Walsh, Panahi spells out his universalism, claiming that all people—not just Iranians and not just women—live within circles of various sizes that limit, to varying degrees, our mobility and freedom. Ultimately he finds the human struggle more interesting, more real, more universal, more glorious, and a more suitable subject for film, than what he thinks of politics.

Whether he likes the title or not, though, Jafar Panahi has become a political figure. He has courageously made films that shine a light on injustice in his country. Since his 2010 arrest he has done so in spite of a six-year prison sentence that is yet to be enforced, always looming over him. Leading up to Iran's 2009 presidential election (which most election experts agree was rigged), he was an outspoken supporter of reformist candidate Mir-Hossein Mousavi; in its aftermath, he championed Mousavi's Green Movement and began production on a movie about it, rumors of which clearly prompted his arrest. Through it all, Panahi has been uncompromising in his patriotism—remaining an Iranian, seeing his work in the context of Iranian film, documenting Iranians in struggle.

As one might expect, he has been reproached in his own country for "political" reasons—and not just by the government. Iranian film criticism (taking after the French, perhaps) is often polemical and confrontational, even in the traditionally deferential format of face-to-face interviews. The results are often illuminating, as in Majid Eslami's and Ahmad Talebinejad's respective interviews, whose hardline questions push the conversation to a new and nuanced level. This robust critical tradition, while surely polemical at times, does not fully account for Panahi's long history of courting controversy. Well before he was on the radar of international festivals or Iran's government, he made his taboo documentary *The Wounded Heads*. Whether refusing to give his fingerprints to US Customs or continuing to make films illegally after having narrowly avoided incarceration, Panahi is intrepid and drawn to controversial subjects. The results, both on- and offscreen, stir controversy in competing, overlapping contexts within Iranian culture, as several interviews and open letters in this volume demonstrate.

The fault lines and sutures that run through Panahi's films are varied, complex, and dichotomous. His films are at once deeply national yet globalized, journalistic yet imaginative, banned in his own country and yet distributed and celebrated around the world. Scholars such as Hamid Naficy, Hamid Dabashi, and Blake Atwood have written extensively on Iranian cinema in the contexts of globalization. In several recent essays, Dabashi suggests that Panahi's career is a case in point of post-national cinema. If Dabashi is right about this, it might explain the questions, repeated by so many interviewers, about whom Panahi really makes his films for. Midway through this volume, Panahi gives a deceivingly simple answer that might be mistaken for canned artist talk, but that, when taken in this context, feels particularly revealing:

"Well, do you make your films for the Iranian audience or not?" asks Massoud Mehrabi.

"No, I make them for myself."

• • •

I was incredibly fortunate to find and work with my assistant editor, Ehsan Khoshbakht. He tracked down vital interviews and writings in Persian without which this volume would be incomplete, and helped me understand in nuanced ways the milieus of Iranian culture and politics. As important, he made contact with Jafar Panahi, who graciously provided us with key pieces in this volume: his early article about working under Abbas Kiarostami, his court defense statement, and the splendid interview he gave for this book. Mr. Panahi was also kind enough to look over the chronology and filmography, updating and correcting both.

To all the translators and interpreters (many of them uncredited), whose invaluable work makes a book like this even possible, I commend you (and envy your bilingualism).

Thanks to my dear friend Bill Fishman, for copyediting the manuscript and offering valuable insights and suggestions.

I am grateful to the editors at the University Press of Mississippi, including Director Craig Gill, Emily Bandy, and Filmmakers in Conversation general editor Gerald Peary (whose volume on John Ford remains an inspiration to this day). They helped make this process a pleasure, offering encouragement and professionalism from the start.

I am much obliged to Kyle Worthington, my teaching assistant par excellence, who picked up the grading slack when it counted the most. I am also indebted to my students at San José State University, who over the years have responded well to Panahi's films and helped me view them from several different perspectives.

This is as good a place as any to express my gratitude for all the film series run by churches and libraries, universities and museums—it was at one of them that I was introduced to Iranian cinema.

This book is lovingly dedicated to my wife Michela and son Max, both of whom survived a year-plus of my blathering about Panahi this and Panahi that.

DT

Chronology

1960	Jafar Panahi is born in Mianeh, Iran, in East Azerbaijan Province, to a working-class, Azeri-speaking family. He is one of seven children, and his father paints houses for a living.
1972–78	By this time Panahi and his family have moved to Tehran, the capital of Iran. At the age of twelve he writes his first book, about a schoolboy who cheats and is caught, winning first prize in a library competition. At the same age, he begins attending movies on his own, against his father's wishes. He later frequents Kanoon, the Institute for the Intellectual Development of Children and Young Adults, where he is exposed to foreign and Iranian movie classics, including Vittorio De Sica's *Bicycle Thieves* and Abbas Kiarostami's *The Bread and Alley*. Throughout his teen years he experiments with photography and makes 8mm short films.
1978–79	The Islamic Revolution succeeds in ousting the American-backed monarchy, replacing it with an Islamic theocracy. In the Islamic Republic of Iran, the new regime targets and highly restricts filmmaking, distribution, and exhibition.
1980–88	After years of tense border relations, the Iran-Iraq War commences shortly after Iran's revolution and lasts for most of the decade. Panahi is conscripted into the Iranian army at the age of twenty, working as an army cinematographer from 1980 to 1982 and shooting war documentaries for Iranian national television (IRIB). In 1981 he is captured by Kurdish rebels and held captive for over two months behind enemy lines. After completing his military service, Panahi enrolls at the College of Cinema and TV (at Iran Broadcasting University) in Tehran, where he studies filmmaking and takes a liking to Alfred Hitchcock, Luis Buñuel, Howard Hawks, and Jean-Luc Godard. In college he makes friends with filmmaker Parviz Shahbazi and cinematographer Farzad Jadat, who would shoot most of Panahi's early films. In 1988, for his thesis project, he directs his first short film, *The Second Look*, which is not released until 1993.

1988–94   After graduating from college, Panahi is contracted to make documentary shorts for Iranian television. These include *The Wounded Heads* (1988), a film he shoots in secret (that would later get banned) about a controversial mourning ritual. In 1992 Panahi makes his first two narrative short films, *The Friend* (1992), inspired by Kiarostami's first short, *The Bread and Alley*, and *The Final Exam*. Both feature nonprofessional actors and win multiple awards at Iran's National TV festival that year. He becomes assistant director for two feature films, first for his friend Kambuzia Partovi (*The Fish*, 1991) and then for his idol and mentor, Abbas Kiarostami (*Through the Olive Trees*, 1994). Kiarostami had seen several of Panahi's short films and hired him when the young filmmaker left a message on his answering machine seeking employment.

1995   Scripted by Kiarostami and featuring nonprofessional actors, Panahi's debut feature film, *The White Balloon*, is released. Though its distribution in Iran is limited to theaters specializing in children's films, his debut enjoys great success abroad. Praised by critics around the world, it goes on to win the Caméra d'Or for best first film at the Cannes Film Festival (among numerous other festival awards). Due to worsening relations with the United States, Iran tries to withdraw the film from consideration by the Academy of Motion Pictures Arts and Sciences and then prohibits Panahi from attending that year's Sundance Film Festival.

1997   Panahi's second feature film, *The Mirror*, is released. Like his debut, this one is about a little girl, and enjoys critical and festival success abroad. He also makes the documentary short *Ardekoul*.

2000   *The Circle*, Panahi's first feature film not starring a child, is released. The Ministry of Culture and Islamic Guidance bans the film in Iran. Without waiting for permission from the Ministry, he submits it to the Venice International Film Festival, where it wins the Golden Lion.

2001   On April 15, in transit from Hong Kong to Buenos Aires, Panahi is detained by customs police at Kennedy Airport and chained to a bench for ten hours. He writes an open letter decrying this treatment, which he feels is based on race and nationality.

2003   *Crimson Gold*, based on real events and scripted by Kiarostami, is released. The Ministry bans it, but once again Panahi submits the film to festivals, and distributes it abroad, without proper permits. At Cannes it wins the Prix Un Certain Regard. Panahi is arrested and interrogated for four hours by the Ministry of Intelligence in Iran.

2006   *Offside* premieres at the Berlin International Film Festival (the Berlinale), where Panahi is awarded the Jury Grand Prix (Silver Bear). Although it is not officially granted distribution rights in Iran, the film is seen widely by Iranians through the dissemination of unlicensed DVDs.

2007   Panahi contributes his single-shot short *Untying the Knot* to the omnibus film *Persian Carpet*.

2009   On June 12 the Islamic Republic of Iran holds its tenth presidential election. Incumbent Mahmoud Ahmadinejad wins in an apparent landslide, but there are irregularities, causing many in and outside of Iran to suspect voting fraud. Millions of Iranians join the Green Movement in support of reformist opposition candidate Mir-Hossein Mousavi and take to the streets to protest the "stolen election." Several protestors, including Mousavi's nephew, are killed and many more are imprisoned. On July 30 Panahi participates in a memorial service for Neda Agha-Soltan, an Iranian protestor killed the month before, and is arrested a second time. The Iranian government releases him after a few days. In September, as head of the jury at the Montreal World Film Festival, he convinces his fellow jurors to wear green scarves in solidarity with the Green Movement in Iran. He applies for a permit to make *Bazgasht* (*Return*), a film about the Iran-Iraq War, but is denied.

2010   On March 1 he is arrested once again, this time taken from his home, along with up to 18 other people (including independent filmmaker Mohammad Rasoulof, members of their film crew, and some family), to Iran's most notorious prison, Evin Prison in Tehran. All but Panahi are released in the days and weeks that follow. Although the government confirms his arrest, no charges are specified. Later that month, fifty Iranian directors, actors, and artists, including Asghar Farhadi, Babak Ahmadi, Mohammad Reza Aslani, Hamid Amjad, Behzad Farahani, Mojtaba Mirtahmasb, Rakhshan Banietemad, Bahram Beyzaie, Kiumars Pourahmad, Naser Taghvai, Mani Haghighi, Leili Rashidi, Homa Rousta, Hamid Samandarian, Khosrow Sinai, Kamran Shirdel, Masoud Kimiai, Fatemeh Motamed-Arya, Khosro Masumi, and Tahmineh Milani, sign a petition calling for his release. The following month, on April 30, American directors, including Paul Thomas Anderson, Martin Scorsese, Steven Spielberg, and the Coen brothers, sign a letter calling for his release. On May 25, after having begun a hunger strike, he is released on $200,000 bail. That same month, the jury at the Cannes Film Festival leaves a chair empty to

	symbolize his absence. On December 20, he is convicted of collusion, assembly, and making propaganda against the Islamic Republic of Iran. He is sentenced to six years in prison, a twenty-year ban on making movies, writing screenplays, giving interviews, and leaving the country (except for the Hajj pilgrimage to Mecca). *The Accordion*, a short, premieres at the 67th Venice International Film Festival as part of Art for The World's THEN AND NOW: Beyond Borders and Differences.
2011	At the 61st Berlinale, Isabella Rossellini reads aloud an open letter penned by Panahi. While awaiting the results of his court appeal, Panahi defies the ban with his first documentary feature, *This is Not a Film*, co-produced with Mojtaba Mirtahmasb. The film is a surprise entry at the 2011 Cannes Film Festival. Later that year it wins the National Society of Film Critics' Best Experimental Film award. On October 15 an Iranian court rejects his appeal and upholds Panahi's sentence.
2012	On October 26, the European Parliament announces that Panahi and Iranian humans rights lawyer Nasrin Sotoudeh will share the Sakharov Prize for Freedom of Thought. Solmaz Panahi accepts the award for her father.
2013	*Closed Curtain*, his second film after the court-imposed ban, premieres at the 63rd Berlin International Film Festival, where he wins the Silver Bear for Best Screenplay. Kambuzia Partovi co-directs and both filmmakers appear in the film.
2014	He wins a Motion Picture Association Asia Pacific Screen Award Academy Film Fund grant ($25,000) for his screenplay *Flower*. Panahi announces he will produce the film and his son will direct it.
2015	*Taxi*, starring Panahi himself, premieres at the 65th Berlin International Film Festival, where it wins the Golden Bear. His niece, Hana Saeidi, who appears in the film, tearfully accepts the award on behalf of her uncle. Also making an appearance in the film is his fellow Sakharov Prize winner Nasrin Sotoudeh.
2016	*Où en êtes-vous, Jafar Panahi?* is commissioned by the Pompidou Center (Paris).
2018	Ahead of its world premiere at the Cannes Film Festival (in select competition for the Palme d'Or), Celluloid Dreams (Paris) acquires world sales rights to Panahi's film *3 Faces*. At Cannes it wins the award for best screenplay (tied with another film).

Filmography

NEGAH-E DOVVOM (THE SECOND LOOK),[1] docudrama short (1988)
Director: **Jafar Panahi**
Cinematography: Farzad Jadat
Editing: **Jafar Panahi**
Sound: Mohammad Ali Abiri
Islamic Republic of Iran Broadcasting (IRIB)—Channel 2
30 mins, 16mm

YARALI BASHAR (THE WOUNDED HEADS), documentary short (1988)
Director: **Jafar Panahi**
IRIB—Channel 2
30 minutes, 16mm

MAHI (THE FISH) (1991)
Director: Kambuzia Partovi
Writing: Kambuzia Partovi
Assistant Director: **Jafar Panahi**
70 minutes

KISH, documentary (1991)
Director: **Jafar Panahi**
IRIB—Channel 2
45 minutes, 16mm

DOUST (THE FRIEND) (1992)
Director: **Jafar Panahi**
Cast: Ali Azizollahi, Mehdi Shahabi
42 minutes, 16mm

AKHARIN EMTEHAN (THE FINAL EXAM), short (1992)
Director: **Jafar Panahi**
Cast: Ali Azizollahi, Mehdi Shahabi

Color
30 minutes, 16mm

ZIRE DERAKHATAN-E ZEYTON (THROUGH THE OLIVE TREES)(1994)
Producers: Alain Depardieu, Abbas Kiarostami
Director: Abbas Kiarostami
Writing: Abbas Kiarostami, Harold Manning (French adaptation), Hengameh
Panahi (French adaptation)
Editor: Abbas Kiarostami
Assistant Director: **Jafar Panahi**

BADKONAK-E SEFID (THE WHITE BALLOON) (1995)
Producers: Kurosh Mazkouri, Foad Nour (IRIB—Channel 2, Ferdos Films, and
the Farabi Cinema Foundation)
Director: **Jafar Panahi**
Writing: Abbas Kiarostami, **Jafar Panahi** (original idea), Parviz Shahbazi (origi-
nal idea)
Cinematography: Farzad Jadat
Production Design: Hamid Reza Ashtianpour, **Jafar Panahi**
Editing: **Jafar Panahi**
Cast: Aida Mohammadkhani (Razieh), Mohsen Kafili (Ali), Fereshteh Sadre
Orafaiy (Aida's mother), Anna Borkowska (old lady), Mohammad Shahani (sol-
dier), Mohammed Bakhtiar (tailor), Aliasghar Smadi (balloon seller), Hamidreza
Tahery (Reza), Asghar Barzegar (pet shop manager), Hasan Neamatolahi (snake
charmer), Bosnali Bahary (snake charmer)
35mm, color, 1.66:1
85 minutes

AYNEH (THE MIRROR) (1997)
Producers: Vahid Nikkhah Azad, **Jafar Panahi** (Rooz Film)
Director: **Jafar Panahi**
Writing: **Jafar Panahi**
Cinematography: Farzad Jadat
Editing: **Jafar Panahi**
Cast: Mina Mohammad Khani (Mina #1), Aida Mohammadkhani (Mina #2),
Kazem Mojdehi, Naser Omuni, M. Shirzad, T. Samadpour
35mm, color, 1.85:1 (hard-matted)
95 minutes

ARDEKOUL, documentary short (1997)
Director: **Jafar Panahi**
Writing: **Jafar Panahi**
29 minutes, color

DAYEREH (THE CIRCLE) (2000)
Producer: **Jafar Panahi** (**Jafar Panahi** Film Productions and Mikado-Lumiere & Co.)
Executive Producer: Morteza Motavali
Director: **Jafar Panahi**
Writing: Kambuzia Partovi, **Jafar Panahi**
Cinematography: Bahram Badakshani
Production Design: Vajid Allah Fariborzi
Art Direction: Iraj Raminfar
Editing: **Jafar Panahi**
Cast: Nargess Mamizadeh (Nargess), Maryiam Palvin Almani (Arezou), Mojgan Faramarzi (Mojgan—prostitute), Elham Saboktakin (Eham—nurse), Monir Arab (Monir—ticket seller), Maedeh Tahmasebi (Maedeh), Maryam Shayegan (Parveneh), Solmaz Panahi (Solmaz), Fereshteh Sadre Orafaiy (Pari)
35mm, color, 1.85:1
90 minutes

TALAYE SORKH (CRIMSON GOLD) (2003)
Producer: **Jafar Panahi** (**Jafar Panahi** Productions)
Director: **Jafar Panahi**
Writing: Abbas Kiarostami
Cinematography: Hossein Jafarian
Production Design: Iraj Raminfar
Editing: **Jafar Panahi**
Music: Peyman Yazdanian
Cast: Hossain Emadeddin (Hussein), Kamyar Sheisi (Ali), Azita Rayeji (the bride), Shahram Vaziri (the jeweler), Ehsan Amani (man in the teahouse), Pourang Nakhael (the rich man), Kaveh Najmabadi (the seller), Saber Safael (the soldier)
35mm, color, 1.66:1
95 minutes

OFFSIDE (2006)
Producer: **Jafar Panahi** (**Jafar Panahi** Film Productions)
Director: **Jafar Panahi**
Writing: **Jafar Panahi**, Shadmehr Rastin

Cinematography: Rami Agami, Mahmoud Kalari
Production Design: Iraj Raminfar
Editing: **Jafar Panahi**
Music: Yuval Barazani, Korosh Bozorgpour
Cast: Sima Mobarak-Shahi (first girl), Shayesteh Irani (smoking girl), Aida Sadeqi (soccer girl), Golnaz Farmani (girl with *chador*), Mahnaz Zabihi (girl disguised as soldier), Nazanin Sediq-zadeh (young girl), Safdar Samandar (soldier from Azerbaijan), Mohammad Kheir-abadi (soldier from Mashad), Masoud Kheymeh-kabood (soldier from Tehran), Hadi Saeedi (soldier), Ali Baradari (bus passenger), Reza Fashani (old man)
35mm, digital video, color, 1.85:1
93 minutes

GEREH-GOSHAII (UNTYING THE KNOT),[2] documentary short (2007)
Director: **Jafar Panahi**
7 minutes

AKKORDEON (THE ACCORDION),[3] short (2010)
Producer: **Jafar Panahi** (Art for The World)
Director: **Jafar Panahi**
Writing: **Jafar Panahi**
Cast: Khadije Bahrami, Kambiz Bahrami
8 minutes

IN FILM NIST (THIS IS NOT A FILM), documentary (2011)
Producers: **Jafar Panahi**, Mojtaba Mirtahmasb
Directors: **Jafar Panahi**, Mojtaba Mirtahmasb
Writing: **Jafar Panahi**, Mojtaba Mirtahmasb
Cinematography: **Jafar Panahi**, Mojtaba Mirtahmasb
Editing: **Jafar Panahi**, Mojtaba Mirtahmasb
Cast: **Jafar Panahi** (himself), Igi (himself, pet lizard), Mojtaba Mirtahmasb (himself), Hasan (himself, part-time janitor)
Digital camcorder, iPhone, color
75 minutes

PARDEH (CLOSED CURTAIN) (2013)
Producer: **Jafar Panahi**,
Executive Producer: Hadi Saeedi
Director: **Jafar Panahi**, Kambuzia Partovi
Writing: **Jafar Panahi**

Cinematography: Mohammad Reza Jahanpanah
Editing: **Jafar Panahi**
Cast: Kambuzia Partovi (writer), Maryam Moqadam (Melika), **Jafar Panahi**
(himself), Hadi Saeedi (Melika's brother), Azadeh Torabi (Melika's sister),
Abolghasem Sobhani (Agha Olia), Mahyar Jafaripour (younger brother), Zeynab
Kanoum (herself)
Digital, color
106 minutes

TAXI (TAXI TEHRAN) (2015)
Producer: **Jafar Panahi** (uncredited) (**Jafar Panahi** Productions)
Director: **Jafar Panahi**
Writing: **Jafar Panahi**
Cinematography: **Jafar Panahi** (Uncredited)
Editing: **Jafar Panahi**
Cast: **Jafar Panahi** (himself, cab driver), Hana Saeidi (herself),[4] Nasrin
Sotoudeh (herself), people in Tehran
Digital, color, 1.78:1
82 minutes

OÙ EN ÊTES-VOUS, JAFAR PANAHI? (WHERE ARE YOU, JAFAR PANAHI?),[5]
(2016)
documentary short
Producer: **Jafar Panahi** (Pompidou Center)
Director: **Jafar Panahi**
Cast: **Jafar Panahi** (himself)
Digital, color
21 minutes

3 FACES (3 ROKH) (2018)
Producer: **Jafar Panahi**
Director: **Jafar Panahi**
Writing: **Jafar Panahi**, Nader Saeivar
Cinematography: Amin Jafari
Editing: Mastaneh Mohajer, Panah Panahi
Production Design: Leila Naghdi Pari
Cast: Behnaz Jafari (herself), **Jafar Panahi** (himself), Marziyeh (herself),
Maedeh Erteghaei (Maedeh), Narges Delaram (mother)
Digital, color
100 minutes

Notes

1. Jafar Panahi indicated to us that this is his debut film (though it wasn't released until 1993). Panahi's thesis film (at the College of Cinema and TV in Tehran) chronicles the making of Kambuzia Partovi's *Golnar*.

2. This single-shot short is one of 15 episodes—each directed by an Iranian filmmaker—that appear in the omnibus film *Persian Carpet*.

3. Commissioned by Art for The World for the THEN AND NOW Beyond Borders and Differences series of short films.

4. Jafar Panahi's niece, who went in place of her uncle to accept the Golden Bear at the 2015 Berlinale.

5. Commissioned by the Pompidou Center (Paris) for its retrospective on Panahi.

Jafar Panahi: Interviews

Notes from the Assistant Director: Kiarostami Has Location Cancer![1]

Jafar Panahi / 1994

From *Film Monthly* (Tehran) 12.168 (December 1994): 108–9. Translated by Shahab Vaezzadeh.

Editor's preface: After directing several shorts and working in television, Jafar Panahi made the transition to feature filmmaking, working under Abbas Kiarostami on his breakthrough film *Through the Olive Trees* (1994). Like no other Iranian production up to that point, *Through the Olive Trees* was distributed widely around the world, enjoying great success on the international film festival circuit. After the film's release, Panahi was invited by *Film Monthly*, post-revolutionary Iran's most prominent film journal, to contribute to a two-part dossier on the production.

•••

"Hello, Mr. Kiarostami. I am Jafar Panahi, a television director. I once made a short film entitled *The Friend (Doust)* that was based on your film *The Bread and Alley (Nan va Koutcheh)*. I read in *Film Monthly* that you want to start making a new film. I would really like to work alongside you in any capacity possible . . ."

Those are the words I used, more or less, when I first left a message on the answering machine. Even after a few days of back-and-forth communication, Kiarostami was still somewhat surprised to see me and my film crew disembark from a minibus opposite the Dorfak Restaurant in Rostamabad, Gilan, on April 7, 1993. Our group settled into a building behind the Dorfak restaurant, which was really the best place that a group of filmmakers could hope to find in all of Rostamabad. I had a chance to read the screenplay that night—a text that Kiarostami did not use even once throughout the process. He had every scene stored in his mind. He recited many screenplays to me during our various trips together after that, perhaps more than ten screenplays that were never written down, yet he had retained all of them in his mind, down to the last detail, in his mind. It is a great pleasure to travel with Kiarostami because he takes every opportunity to describe different screenplays and one wonders when they will ever be made.

I don't remember exactly how I came to realize that diligence is one of the most important factors in earning his trust. When working with Kiarostami, it does not matter whether you are a professional or an amateur. What matters is that you have complete confidence in the work that you do and that he senses that confidence within you.

I met Kiarostami, Saba, and Samakbashi[2] the next day, and together we headed towards the village of Koker in our Nissan Patrol. I saw the hill that marked the start of the road to Koker in Kiarostami's 1987 film *Where Is the Friend's Home?* (*Khane-ye Doust Kodjast?*).[3] The lone tree stood firm on top of the hill, but it looked bare and was not as beautiful as it had appeared in the film. Nevertheless, it was still a sufficient setting for a child running along its elegant road in search of a friend, and, some distance away, for an old man to sit under, talking about his weekly pocket money and the beating he receives every fifteen days.

We arrived in Koker, at the grandmother's house. We exited the car. Kiarostami told me several times what I had to do in order to prepare the location. We had agreed that I would prepare the site with the help of a few crew members, but the details had not yet been finalized. And so, more reminders—even after he got into the car with Saba and Samakbashi and drove away, he turned around and came back to reiterate the same points for the umpteenth time. I walked up, reassured him, and asked him to give me until four o'clock. When he returned in the afternoon, everything that he wanted had been delivered and I had gained his trust.

Filming started at the grandmother's house the next day. I had always assumed that Kiarostami gave his amateur actors the freedom to make up their own dialogue. I observed, however, that all of the film's dialogue came from Kiarostami himself. He tactfully fed lines to the actors whenever he had a quiet moment alone with them so that they would forget the boundary between his dialogue and their own. Using his knowledge of different social classes, professions, and people, he speaks to his actors in their own language and dialect. He does not simply invent dialogue; he compiles it. He knows, for example, what Hossein would say in a certain situation given his character traits, or what Mahbanou might have to say, given her age. The actors therefore recite the dialogue in their own language and dialect, with minor adjustments to certain words. One can easily imagine how this differs from other films.

It became clear from day one that Kiarostami is never bound by the vision that he has constructed in his mind. Despite already having a complete outline of his vision, he remains open-minded on set, so that he can easily communicate the feeling that has been established in a scene by giving weight to its strong and powerful images. The weight given to those images is sometimes stretched to the brink of madness. Kiarostami has location cancer; that is the best way I can put it! He continues to look for suitable angles, images, and new locations until the last day. He was overcome with joy, like a schoolboy when his teacher hasn't shown up to class, whenever there was a break in filming due to poor weather or whatever the reason may have been. He would take the opportunity to hop into his Nissan Patrol in search of a new location. He believes that everything happens for a reason, and therefore whenever he is not able to film something on a certain day, it must mean that something better is waiting to be found elsewhere.

I will never forget the day that he captured the gypsy girl's bashful smile as she sat in the back of the pickup truck beside Zahra. We hadn't been able to film anything for three days due to weather conditions, but his eyes lit up with joy, and he believed that if another three days passed without being able to film anything, he would still be happy with that one shot. Strangely enough, even with all of the breaks and disruptions, filming was wrapped up in less than two months: forty-five days for the first stint, and then another fifteen days in Rostamabad with a handful of crew members to capture a few final shots and retake others that had been damaged in the editing studio.

After preparing the grandmother's house, it was time for the film's first sequence. Don't get the wrong idea when I say "time"—no precise or definite plans can be made when working with Kiarostami. He may stare at an actor's face one morning and sense that the actor is ready to film a specific sequence, in which case all plans must be dropped and the crew must prepare for a new sequence.

Work began with Keshavarz.[4] Keshavarz knew exactly how to work with Kiarostami. He understood that to be successful, he would have to forget his decades of experience as a film and stage actor, and surrender himself completely to the will of Kiarostami. That gave him a strange sense of fear in the beginning. I don't know if "fear" is the right word, but the anxiety and trepidation hidden beneath his smile on the shoot was quite plain to see. The first shot was done in just two takes, which was quite unbelievable given that it was thirty seconds long, and Keshavarz managed to breathe a sigh of relief after that. Due to his background in cinema, there were several occasions during the two months of filming when he did not feel as comfortable as the amateur actors did in front of the camera. However, he would always persist and try to perform as the other actors did.

We were in the middle of filming for the sequence at the groom's house when we noticed that Keshavarz had been sitting with Hossein Jafarian and seemed a little too happy. Even after filming a few takes, he was still in high spirits. At that point we decided to play a trick on him that we had devised earlier. Kiarostami declared, "I'll read Hossein's dialogue. Panahi, you get the shot. Everyone ready:

Keshavarz, Jafarian, Karimi, Ansarian. Lights, camera, action!" But even after the sixth take, Keshavarz's mood hadn't changed. As planned, I was then supposed to voice my anger with Keshavarz, which I did (although it was a little more scathing than Kiarostami and I had agreed upon). Keshavarz's mood dropped and we managed to film a take that Kiarostami was happy with. Afterwards, I tried to reconcile with Keshavarz while Kiarostami acted as mediator. "I knew it was a trick!" Keshavarz said, laughing.

It has just occurred to me that I'm supposed to be writing an article—but should it be a report or a memoir? I don't know whether I should include this incident or not. It would be a shame not to mention Saba and Kiarostami's long-standing friendship, and the dispute they had on that particular warm day. The weather was intensely hot. I don't think we ever experienced more torturous weather throughout the time we spent filming.

I would like to put an end to all of the rumors surrounding the incident by explaining what really happened. Anyone who works in cinema knows that disagreements between professionals on all different levels are unavoidable while filming. It is entirely possible for much more hostile disputes to occur on the shoot without really impacting the production process. Their dispute was so trivial and meaningless that it could have very easily been resolved. But of course, because Kiarostami and Saba were such good friends, the solution they decided upon was the best one possible: to go on with a different cinematographer.

If I continue like this, this article will turn into a book. And I could never hope to write a better book than Kiumars Pourahmad's *Where Is the Friend's Home?*[5] So: CUT!

Next: The weather was probably the biggest cause of disruption to film production, and it continued to flaunt its power until the very last day. After production was wrapped up on June 8, 1993 and the film crew sent back to Tehran, Kiarostami and I paid another visit to the filming locations. We settled payments and concluded business with locals who had contributed to the film and then made our way back to Tehran. It was then the weather's turn to play one last trump card . . .

Flashback: While visiting filming locations during the early days of production, we arrived in a new region and Kiarostami asked me to close my eyes. A couple of minutes later, the car came to a halt. Kiarostami exited the vehicle, opened my door, took my hand, and gently led me to the side of the road. I was then given permission to open my eyes—and there was the beautiful field of olive trees from the film's final scene. Kiarostami visited that location several times after that, in order to find the best angles. We also returned there a few times to film. He wanted the wind to blow and clouds to pass intermittently across the sun, so that he could frame those two white dots in one magnificent long shot. The wind blew, but the sun and the clouds were not so cooperative. Our attempts to capture the shot on different days also proved fruitless.

Moving on: We had just passed the city of Manjil when an enormous rainbow began to form just a few steps in front of us. You could almost reach out and grab it. After that, we passed the city of Lowshan, where rays of sunlight flickered through the clouds and across the vast plains. A heavy silence followed; there were no words. Not even a screenplay could have described it.

Notes

1. This playful (and, for some readers, distasteful) title, which appeared on the cover of the magazine, stirred controversy upon its publication. The filmic use of the word "location" does not exist in Farsi, so only those who had been on a film set understood the reference. Many readers were led to believe that Kiarostami had an obscure type of cancer, an impression which the magazine corrected in the following edition. (Several decades later, in 2016, Kiarostami died of gastrointestinal cancer.)
2. Cinematographer Farhad Saba and sound engineer Mahmoud Samakbashi.
3. *Where Is the Friend's Home?* is the first of Kiarostami's Koker trilogy, so named because all three films are set in Koker, a village in northern Iran. The other two titles in the trilogy are *Life, and Nothing More...* (1992) and *Through the Olive Trees* (1994).
4. Mohammad-Ali Keshavarz, veteran stage and screen actor who appeared in several key films of the first Iranian New Wave.
5. Pourahmad's book details the making of this film.

Discovering the Charm of Secondary People: *The White Balloon*

Omid Rouhani / 1995

From: *Film Monthly* (Tehran) 13.171 (1995¹): 159–160. Translated by Katayoun Youssefi.

Omid Rouhani : Did you work out your own plot or did Abbas Kiarostami write the script? If so, what attracted you to his script?

Jafar Panahi: I started with a brief sketch and spent a lot of time working on it before passing it to Kiarostami. In this sketch the focus was on the events and narrative; but after Kiarostami wrote the script it was the characters in supporting roles that came to the foreground—the people who couldn't attend the New Year's Eve festivities, each for their own reason. Each situation seemed to me like a painting. So the story of losing the money and buying fish became an excuse for standing in front of this painting and looking at it.

OR: Do you consider yourself a director of children's films, or did you just get involved in it by chance?

JP: I really don't know. Up until now, whenever I decided to make a film, either short film or feature film or documentary, it has ended up featuring a child. In *The Wounded Heads,* my documentary about the ritual of *Qama Zani,*[2] I pass through the ceremony in different directions and arrive at a child who is holding a sword above his head and trying to imitate the rest. Here it ends in a freeze frame and we see the closing credits. I don't know, maybe it is nothing more than childhood memories. Maybe I can work on other subjects when I'm through with my childhood. But in fact, I don't think that will ever happen.

OR: In your film, again, we see realism. Is realism important for you? Though the reality that you depict is not harsh. All the characters are very kind and supportive. Isn't that at odds with reality?

JP: Talking about reality is a mistake! There isn't such a thing as reality in cinema.

How can we define the limits of such a reality? We are arranging everything from the beginning. Even by choosing the lens we are manipulating the reality. It's not my fault if the spectator wants to ignore the fact that he came to the cinema and paid to be entertained. It is his own problem that he doesn't want to accept the reality. But this point you make about "kind people" is very interesting. At the Children Film Festival in Isfahan[3] there were many objections, including that there isn't any nice person in the film, except for the Armenian woman.[4] I think you have to ask them about it.

OR: Was the sequence of events in the script the way we see it, in order to make the film appealing and engaging, or did you change the order of events?
JP: Yes, it is exactly as it reads in the script, but just to the point where the man who sells balloons appears at the end of the film. In fact, first we thought, we'll have an old man play this role. But as I said before, what attracted me to this script was the odd supporting roles. So I looked for the strangest options. When I saw this Afghan boy in the streets of a suburb of Tehran by chance, I realized that he should be the one, and since he is almost Ali's age, first they could start to fight and then make up in a silly and childish play. This argument and its following friendship caused some changes to the screenplay. Now I had no control over the rest of the film. Everything changed with this Afghan boy. In the screenplay, the film was supposed to end like this: Ali and Raziye run towards the fish seller and are disappointed when they realize that the shop is closed; an old man who sits beside the fish seller gives them the fishbowl. I shot the whole scene. But in the editing room, it didn't appeal to me anymore. The Afghan boy had influenced everything and it was impossible to forget him. I thought to myself that I didn't care if these kids buy fish or not, or if the shop is closed or not; I was interested in the supporting roles in the first place. So I ended the film with him. Even the name of the film was changed under his influence, from *Happy New Year* to *The White Balloon*.

OR: Did you try to keep the cinematic time in parallel with the real time? Apparently the timing was carefully calculated and was included in the shooting script. But did you really have a shooting script?
JP: Honestly when we were shooting the film, I didn't bother with this. Then in the recording studio, when the voice on the radio announces the time left till the New Year, it is actually the time of the film as well. That is, we hear that one hour and eighteen minutes is left until the New Year, which is almost the time that is left in the film at that moment. Although this was only true with the version that was screened in Isfahan, because after that festival I cut five minutes of the film.

But the story of the shooting script is different. When I was studying at the university, I thought that I had to specify every detail before shooting. So I had a form for every single issue and clarified everything from different angles. But I felt that the short films I made during that period were not alive, were very formal and rigid. Actors moved around like objects, very inflexible and stiff. So I came to the conclusion that I needed to release myself. Not to abandon the shooting script completely, but to build the structure of the project in a way that welcomes the changes that appear during the process.

OR: How did you work with the children?

JP: Working with children (or amateur actors in general) can be both easy and difficult. And both for the same reason: Their unfamiliarity with the camera. But as soon as they accept the camera and get used to it they treat it much more professionally than the professional actors. However, the right choice of actors is the basis of everything. I believe that everybody is an actor and if they play in a role that matches their character, they can handle it easily. But you have to believe that in all Iran there is just one person who can play that role. Your task is looking for that particular person. When you have the right person, it will be easier to work with them. I found Aida easily, but not Ali. I brought the soldier from Neyshabour and the fish seller from Rasht. First, I usually try to build a friendship, which is very helpful. Your happiness makes them happy and they get sad with your sadness. If you want them to cry, you just need to pretend to be sad. They burst into tears. This is only one way among thousands. You have many options, and here the actor's character is crucial. Aida is smart; soon I realized that she would do anything we had agreed on. So we agreed on this: whenever I asked her to cry, she just needed to look into my eyes and cry. In the first days, we looked at each other and we both cried. Later on, it was enough for her to look at me and weep alone, just like that.

OR: When you were working with children, did you film everything in a single shot or did you go through everything several times?

JP: The first take is the best one, and children are usually the best in that first take. If you are lucky and everything goes well, nothing interferes with the camera or sound or light. Sometimes it happens that you shoot a scene ten times, but cannot stop thinking about that first take. Practice doesn't make sense when working with children. As much as possible, I do not even let them know the story of the film. The actor is the first person who sees the film scene by scene. She goes through the story as she plays the role. In each scene she naturally reacts to the situation, and as the whole experience is new for her, she is very eager to proceed and see where the sequence ends. But if she goes through rehearsals, she doesn't react naturally, she just pretends the role.

OR: In your film, as Kiarostami has also mentioned, much of this purity and reality and naturalness come from the sound of the film. How did you work with sound?

JP: People who watched the film pointed to the proper use of sound. Even Marco Mueller[5] told me that this film was the only film in which he tried not to use translator headphones, to be able to hear the background sound better. He talked a lot about the effect of these sounds. But I am not happy with the sound, because I didn't have enough time to work on it. Maybe I should think of a sound designer for the next films. Sound could be deeply effective.

Notes

1. Several Iranian interviews included in this volume are listed without the month (or season), because they were published according to the Persian calendar, which is difficult to translate precisely to the Gregorian calendar.

2. Known in Arabic as *tatbir,* this is an act of mourning by Shia Muslims in Iran and other countries that commemorates the massacre of Hussein ibn Ali, grandson of the prophet Muhammad, and his family and supporters at the Battle of Karbala (680 CE). The practice, which involves ritual blood-letting, is traditional but controversial and, in Iran, illegal.

3. Isfahan, Iran's third-largest city, has long hosted this popular festival devoted to films about and/or for youth.

4. Because most Iranian Christians are of Armenian descent, there is a tendency in Iran to call all Christians "Armenians." The kind Christian woman in the film is in fact played by Anna Borkowska, who, before she passed away in 2008, was one of the last surviving Polish refugees to settle in Iran during World War II. Panahi correctly notes her Polish heritage in a later interview in this volume

5. Then-director of the Locarno Film Festival.

Empathy and Understanding

Film Monthly / 1995

From *Film Monthly* (Tehran) 13.174 (1995): 23–24. Translated by Katayoun Youssefi.

Another wonder for Iranian cinema, *The White Balloon* won the Caméra d'Or at Cannes, the International Critics Prize, and the Confederation of Art and Experiments Award. Yet considering the great success Iranian films have enjoyed in international festivals the last few years, it could hardly be called an exception. Maybe it's time to accept that the world loves Iranian cinema. We talked to Panahi, mainly to glean all we could about Cannes and the film's reception there. We leave our questions about the film itself to another occasion, maybe after its public screening.

Film Monthly: How did you get your debut film entered into Cannes?
Jafar Panahi: After Fajr Film Festival[1] there were some requests from other festivals, like Locarno, where we planned for its premiere. Then we realized that Cannes was another possibility, which made Marco Mueller, the director of the Locarno Film Festival, upset.

FM: Tell us about the screening and the audience's reactions.
JP: We arrived in Cannes the day before the screening, and it was my first trip abroad. My friends advised me not to go to the press screening of the film, which was in the morning of the second day of the festival. They said that normally, critics and journalists react coldly and hide their admirations. Directors prefer not to go to such meetings; it may make them less confident. I went, though a bit late. The hall was packed, to the point where we had to sit on the floor. The film started, and the reception was very good. No one left the room, and when it ended, there was great applause. This was a good beginning. The reception was good again in the evening, which was the public screening. It coincided with an important film from another category. A few of the well-known critics and journalists came to *The White Balloon* instead of the other film, as a result of word of mouth from the

morning screening. The next morning the positive reviews started rolling in, and with all the demands, instead of seven screenings, as was originally planned, the film got ten screenings. In those small rooms with twenty-five seats, a director would be happy if three to four people stayed till the end of the film. But for *The White Balloon* people were seated on the floor and they went for an additional screening.

FM: What do you think is the reason for such a positive reception?

JP: I think it is related to Iranian cinema in general. We should find the reason why they are so eager for Iranian films. The fact is that no one out there knew me; it was enough for them to know the film is Iranian. Part of it comes from the Farabi Cinema Foundation that organizes everything so well. They have learned over the years how they should send the films; each film goes to the appropriate category where it has the best chance. This film could fit in any category, but they decided on the Directors' Fortnight, which was right. Showing the film in the first days of the festival was another key decision that helped its success. The film created a sensation in those first days. But the second reason is the fact that our great cinematic figures paved the way for us. If I know anything, I learned it from their films, from Beyzaie, Kimiai, Taghvai, Mehrjui, Naderi, and particularly Kiarostami, whose work has long interested me. Their films were an introduction, or a background for Iranian cinema, which has become so powerful now. We had a small sample out there, but it shined. Everybody wanted to know more about Iranian cinema, and we can't ignore the role of these filmmakers in creating a strong foundation for current Iranian cinema.

FM: Which aspects appealed more to the foreign audience: the social-political aspects, the film's formal approach, or the nonprofessional actors?

JP: Like many others, I thought maybe political issues regarding Iran or talking about poverty attracted the foreign audience. But this was not the case. Among the subjects discussed in interviews, it was mostly the humanist sensibility present in Iranian films that attracted them. For example, they pointed to the soldier who didn't carry any weapon, who had no intention to kill.

This aspect is also mentioned in the award by the international critics: making films that approach human issues with empathic understanding and depth. They talked about "political commitment" when they gave the Critics' Prize to Ken Loach; "sensitivity to contemporary social issues" also was mentioned in reference to Angelopoulos' film, the other winner. While there are many films that discuss poverty, it is mostly a humanistic approach that attracted the festival. We are making a cultural image of ourselves with these films and we affect people's attitudes towards us. After one of the screenings of the film, in a place far from

Cannes, an old lady asked me about *Not Without My Daughter.*[2] She thought it had a different atmosphere, and there wasn't any pool with fish in the houses in that film. I explained to her that this is part of Persian architecture, and I told her about the goldfish in *Haft Sin*.[3] I reminded her that *Not Without My Daughter* was not made by an Iranian, and it was not shot in Iran. Some foreign films made about Iran sometimes give false impressions about us, and our films can change people's opinions. I think even the worst Iranian films can have a positive effect. In Cannes they didn't see us as representative of a developing country, but as a cinematic power.

FM: What was the reaction of Iranians?

JP: It was very good. They were proud of it. An old lady was saying that she doesn't want to see any other Iranian film after this, because she wants to preserve the memory of this film for the rest of her life. "I want to believe that Iran is this," she told me, "that the cinema of Iran is this. I want to keep all of these memories in my mind."

FM: Which other festivals planned to show the film?

JP: Many festivals have asked us, but the fact is that after an A-level festival, you can't show it in some other festivals. At the moment, showings are planned in Tokyo, Turin, and São Paulo.

FM: When will the public screening be?

JP: I don't know yet. I hope TV doesn't show it before the screening.

Let me say something about TV now. When I finished at the College of Cinema and TV, I went to Bandar Abass and there I made some short films, which won a prize in the Film and TV Festival. Then I returned to Tehran and worked for Channel One for three years and couldn't do anything else. Everything I proposed to the children's department, they rejected. I even told them, Give me your worst schemes and I'll make something out of them. But they didn't let me. When I moved to Channel Two, they accepted the same scheme that was rejected by Channel One. The people in Channel Two have better knowledge and understanding. There are many people like me who would work better in a system with better management. I hope *The White Balloon* encourages the directors to create such opportunities for others.

FM: What is your next project?

JP: Most likely I start next year. I would like to work with television again, although there are some opportunities in the private sector as well. But I'm interested in television and it is true that I don't have to worry about the financial issues there.

FM: Again children?

JP: Again children. Maybe because my main concern is still my own childhood.

Notes

1. This is considered the most important of several annual state-sponsored film festivals in Iran, held on the anniversary of the Iranian Revolution.
2. Brian Gilbert's 1991 film about an American woman (played by Sally Field) and her daughter trying to escape Islamic Iran (and her ruthless husband, who lures his family on vacation to his homeland and secretly plans for them to stay).
3. Traditional Iranian New Year table display comprised of seven foods, each one starting with the letter *sin* in the Persian alphabet.

A Conversation with Jafar Panahi: Cinema without Emphasis

Majid Eslami and Houshang Golmakani / 1996

From *Film Monthly* (Tehran) 13.181 (1996): 44–47. Translated by Philip Grant.

Houshang Golmakani: When *The White Balloon* was finished, did you foresee these kinds of positive reactions, this kind of success?

Jafar Panahi: To be honest, no, because this was a first project for most members of the crew, and when we were making it our only thought was to get it done. It was only when the film got into the Children Film Festival in Isfahan that everyone began to think things were getting serious. Before that we didn't think it at all. Then it was only at Fajr Film Festival where we got to see the film all cleaned up, because at Isfahan the conditions for screening were poor and you couldn't hear the sound properly. We worked on the sound again for Fajr and when it was screened there, that was the first time I was really satisfied with it.

A few days ago I was on the set of Abbas Kiarostami's film and someone asked me what had changed about me. And I answered, "Nothing," because I was just as I had been when I had worked as an assistant on the set of *Through the Olive Trees*. But afterwards I thought about it and realized that the only change in me was that I'd become more self-confident. Because that was my first film and I didn't know exactly how my ideas would turn out in practice, whereas these days I'm sure about that. For example, in the scene where the neighbor's son comes to sell his fish to the fishmonger, the usual way in which you'd get the audience to understand what is going on would be to have a close-up of the boy and another of the girl, and then show them looking at one another. And on set my colleagues told me that the boy appeared in the corner of the frame and his image was too small and couldn't be seen. I said that the audience would have to understand what was going on based on all of the hints we gave them. They'd have to have an image of the character in their mind. So they said, "Very well, take a close-up anyway, and if, when it comes to the editing, you don't want to use it, you don't have to, but if you don't take it now you won't be able to do anything about it afterwards." One of the focus pullers always used to say, "Put some inserts in at the end of the tape, perhaps you'll need them later." During the filming of that scene he said, "You never take any inserts, come and get this one." I said that what we had was enough, that we didn't need anything else. And then wherever in the world we screened the film, at that very moment people in the audience started talking to the people next to them, and everyone thought they were the one who'd discovered it. At the time, what I did was the sort of thing a student would do, but now that I've seen the result, my self-confidence has increased a lot. I think we can count on the audience, we can believe in their intelligence.

Majid Eslami : In any case, what does it matter if the viewers don't get it the first time round? As it happens, I think *The White Balloon* is one of those films that however many times you watch it you still discover something new. That's not a weakness in the film, and it's not a weakness in the viewer. It's fantastic that the film is still alive when you see it for the umpteenth time.

HG: Following up on the example you gave, it's clearer in the scene with the fishmonger than in the scene by the pool in the courtyard. In the latter it works so subtly that at the end of the day you don't know whether the boy has caught two fish or more. When did he catch them anyway? Because we didn't see it.

ME: When Ali asks, "How many did you get?" what did you do to make the feeling more intense?

JP: Here again we played around with the sound. I thought that the sound of the wood hitting the colander and the bucket would stay in the viewer's mind. I told myself that if it's possible to use these sounds when the girl is walking, then the audience will start to have doubts. But I haven't heard those sounds in any copies of the film.

ME: But now that the sound isn't there, more doubt is produced in the viewer's mind.

HG: The viewers think to themselves, "Who made this sound? The one we didn't even hear!"

JP: When it comes to sound, for a while I worked with someone who believed that a good sound was one that could be heard, but I would say that if it were necessary, it would be heard. My belief is that the level of a sound should be what it would be naturally. That means that if we are open to hearing it, we will hear it.

ME: In your work before *Through the Olive Trees*, in your short films, did you have the same notions about sound emerging naturally out of the spaces you shot?

JP: In those films I didn't have the self-confidence I do now. Because I didn't have any technical knowledge when it came to sound, I usually passed on that stage of filmmaking. I was experimenting with something in every one of those films: getting a performance out of actors, cutting, and so on. That's why when it came to the point in the process where we'd work on the sound, I'd pass on it. For that reason I no longer feel very friendly towards my film *The Friend*, because I wasn't able to record the sound on set and so had to go with ADR, and the voices sound awful. But *The Final Exam* is a bit better as far as sound quality goes. In any case, at the time, I didn't have any technical knowledge about sound recording. The experience of *Through the Olive Trees* was extraordinary, however, because I understood that it's not necessary to get each and every single technical detail of sound recording; instead what matters is to grasp the meaning every sound can have and how it might be felt.

HG: To what extent were the uncertainty and lack of clarity in the film already in the script?

JP: What do you mean by that exactly?

HG: I mean, were you thinking from the very beginning that you would not emphasize the things that other films do?

JP: The truth is that I really don't know. Some things were in the script, some things were decided on set. When I first told Abbas Kiarostami about the scenario for the film, he didn't then go off and write the script; rather, he started telling the story to me.

HG: Was the initial treatment yours?

JP: It was mine and Parviz Shahbazi's.

ME: How long was it?

JP: About ten pages. In the original treatment we were after plot, and less interested in things incidental to the story; it was Abbas Kiarostami who brought us that. Originally at the end of the film the camera was supposed to follow Razieh and her brother to the fishmonger's. We even shot that footage, but I didn't use it because it occurred to me that following the two of them wouldn't have added anything to the film and that I should stick with the Afghan boy at the end.

ME: When it comes to acting, it looks like your approach to performance differs from Kiarostami's. Especially when it comes to Aida.

JP: My approach varies depending on the person. It really depends on which method is most likely to succeed. When it came to Aida, often I'd play the role and then she'd imitate what I did. But when it came to the snake charmers, I couldn't act out the parts myself. I just had to leave them free to do what they wanted, or to make them angry so that they would get into the right frame of mind.

ME: What about the tailor?

JP: He had been a tailor for forty years. I didn't want anything particular out of him; I just had to make sure he was doing the right thing. After a couple of rehearsals, it all turned out how I wanted. For example, the things he said when he was next to the tree—"He doesn't even have ten *shahis* in his pocket"—this scene we had been filming for two days and it just wouldn't work. Then I realized that this man was sensitive about people in the neighborhood seeing him, because that was where he worked every day. So I made sure there'd always be a few people around him so that he'd get even angrier. You just have to see what will work with each person and what the limits of their abilities are. There's no single formula. Everyone is sensitive to something. For instance, for Aida, it was a big deal to get an eraser; she had a collection of erasers and that was something we were really able to use.

ME: She wasn't difficult at all?

JP: No, at first she was very good and cooperated well. Then she spilled boiling water on herself and we had to suspend filming for twenty days. After that she toyed with us a little bit. We didn't talk for a day or two, and I told her that I'd go and get her classmate to play the role in her place. She went home and said, "That's what he thinks! But he won't find anyone better than me to play the role." So she knew what we were like, and I had to give her an eraser or two so that she would cooperate.

ME: Was the idea of different ethnic groups there in the original script?

JP: No, actually. Instead of the Armenian woman there was a different woman, but the soldier on the other hand was always from Neyshabour. The boy who sells balloons was also not originally Afghan. And the tailor just happened to be Azeri.[1] When we were choosing the location we saw that there was a tailor's shop nearby and the tailor was Azeri. The fishmonger was Rashti[2] because that was appropriate given his profession. And then I thought to myself, "Now that these people have been selected, wouldn't it be fun if the balloon seller were an Afghan, to accentuate his strangeness."

Incidentally, something happened on set that was related to this mixing of different ethnic groups. We filmed the sequence with the snakes in an old Tehran neighborhood. We had found the location after a thousand difficulties, but then we found out that there was a local authority whose permission you needed even to drink water in the neighborhood. He had taken a dislike to us and wouldn't let us work. Everyone advised us not to get in a fight with him. In the end I went up to him and said to him in Azeri, "Look, you're Azeri, I'm Azeri. If you like, kill me, but we'll get on with our work." When he saw how stubborn we were, he kissed my face and didn't utter a word after that!

ME: What about the dialogue, was it exactly as it was in the script?

JP: For example, the dialogue with the soldier was exactly like that. Aida had memorized everything and when the soldier forgot his lines she'd even remind him of them. We could say that about ninety percent of the dialogue was as it was in the script.

HG: The vagueness of the soldier's second reason for returning home made me wonder whether his hanging around in that neighborhood, with nothing to do, was because he was waiting to meet someone.

JP: No, that's not what I was thinking. When I was a soldier myself in the town of Ajab Shir that's how it was. When we had a few hours to ourselves, we went to the public baths and then walked around the town. At the beginning of the film, when the soldier gets out of the jeep, we hear two honks of the horn and somebody says something and he replies that he understands, as if he's arranging to meet them. Then we see the same people come to pick him up and they complain to him that they spent three hours looking for him.

ME: Of course it's the vagueness that sets the mind thinking.

HG: If we were to ask you yourself what the second reason was, you'd tell us you didn't know either!

JP: Perhaps he *was* waiting for someone. In any case, I don't know. I didn't ask him and he didn't tell me! In Japan they asked what Ali said to persuade his mother to give him the money. I replied that I had been with Razieh in the courtyard and I hadn't heard what he said because of the sound of a vacuum cleaner! They asked me whether I hadn't asked Ali what he'd said, and I told them that I had but that he had said it was a secret between him and his mother. All I'd said to Ali was that if he could persuade his mother to give him the money, he'd have a reward from me. I gave him his reward, but he never told me how he persuaded his mother! And they thought that in Iran that's really how we make films!

ME: Was the father purposely kept hidden in the script?

JP: Yes. As it happens, the father who is in the bathroom is Aida's father. The entire family's in the film: The person who picks up the vase is Aida's sister, the woman who tells her to come here so she can buy her a fish is in fact Aida's mother. I worked a lot on the tone and level of the father's voice so it'd be on the border of being heard and not heard.

HG: In this kind of film, given what we see and hear of the father, we assume he is a rough or violent father.

JP: I don't see any violence. The deal is that the father has two jobs, that's his family situation, and he has to go and pick up the mother. Last year he didn't do that and she's been complaining about it. It's *Nowruz*, Iranian New Year's Day, and the son has bought soap instead of shampoo. The way he behaves is completely natural. In the same way we cannot assume the tailor is a violent man. There's no time for discussion and argument because everyone is in a rush to get things done.

ME: To what extent were you intent upon portraying child workers?[3] Because they are everywhere. Or rather, they are both there and not there. For example, the tailor's apprentice is fascinating. The exchange of glances, then the scene where he takes his leave.

JP: The tailor's apprentice wasn't in the script. With the Afghan boy, I was trying to make the group of children more complete. The truth is that it has something to do with my own past and the ways I experienced diversity as an adolescent. That boy was working in the next-door pastry shop. We brought him in to play this role. The scene where he takes his leave is a custom of theirs; the boy has to be the first one to extend his hand and receive his New Year's present.

HG: Can you explain how you organized the filming for the first shot?

JP: The location was in Kashan, and it gave me a lot of room for maneuvering. When we found the location, we had to set up everything: the *kokoretsi*[4] seller, the greengrocer, etc. Most of the extras were students, and we added a few others to them. I think we shot the scene in six takes. Our shoot began with that scene, in fact. Apart from a couple of shots we did to get Aida used to the camera, we were just trying stuff out.

ME: So you made things very difficult for yourself by bringing most of the actors together in the first scene, because if one of them had left later on, during filming, or hadn't been able to continue, everything would have fallen apart, or at the very least you'd have had to reshoot that complicated first sequence.

JP: Well, we had everyone's address, and we had made agreements with all of them. For that shot, we took everyone to Kashan.

HG: The young Afghan man was also in that shot. You said you found him during the course of filming.

JP: No, I found him when I was selecting my actors. When I saw that my selections tended to bring together actors from different ethnic groups, I decided to pick him as well, for the role of the balloon seller.

HG: Did you imagine that the young man from Neyshabour could have been anything other than a soldier? Why did you choose a soldier?

JP: Military service is a period of exile in a person's life. If I had chosen someone else, the feeling of exile would not have been nearly so great. Military service is usually the first feeling of exile anyone has in their life, and for ordinary people, it is the first time they have been far away from their families.

HG: Did you work a lot on the sound? Did work on it take as long as the actual shooting?

JP: Longer. Before Mehdi Dezhbodi got to work on the sound, I had already edited the sound recordings, during the break between the two shoots when Aida scalded herself. Afterwards, Mehdi Dezhbodi and I worked an awful lot on little details to do with the sound, and it went on until a few days before the opening of the Children Film Festival in Isfahan. I think that we worked on the sound for as long as we worked on shooting and editing the film combined.

HG: Had you made up your mind from the very beginning not to have any music?

JP: No, that was the result of inexperience when we started. I had in fact commissioned a score from Farshid Rahmanian, because I thought that a film needs music. But then when he played me the music, I thought that it wasn't really right for the film. He went away and wrote some more music. When he came back with that, I realized that the problem wasn't whether this music was any good or not; I saw that I had been mistaken and that the film didn't need music at all, and that the best soundtrack I could have for the film was background noise. Farshid Rahmanian had gone to great trouble, twice over, but it was my mistake, my inexperience, that meant that I didn't realize initially that the film had no need for music.

HG: You mean, after all the work you'd put in on the sound, you concluded that your film didn't need music?

JP: No, I figured out that the sound needed more work when we were halfway through editing. I was gradually making progress and thinking about what sorts of things could be done with the sound—for instance, the sound of the radio. We started filming on April 5, 1994, but a little earlier, on *Nowruz*,[5] I had recorded the New Year's programs off the radio to use in the film. When I started working on it, however, I saw that the recording wouldn't synchronize with the images. So I timed each scene that had the radio playing, and I got hold of some radio announcers and got them to read sentences the length of each scene to imply the passing of time.

HG: The film was screened at Isfahan last year, but at the end of the film it says 1374.[6]

JP: Because we knew the film would come out in 1995, from the beginning we had *Nowruz* 1374 in mind.

ME: At the time, this produced an interesting feeling in the audience, because we felt that the action of the film was happening in the future. Now the feeling is different.

JP: We went and researched the starting time of *Nowruz* in 1995,[7] and we saw that it would be after midnight, but we couldn't shift the action of the film to that time of night. The action was set at dusk, so the time of day doesn't correspond to the timing of *Nowruz* 1995.

HG: You could have had it so that the 'four' at the end of 1374 wouldn't be heard, so you wouldn't hear the sound of the announcer telling us it's New Year. It could have been covered by another sound.

ME: I don't remember exactly how the last shot was in the Isfahan version. All I remember is that it was different, but I think that the ending you have now is much better.

JP: I thought about this a lot. One way of ending it that occurred to me was to make that moment last longer, as they do on TV when, at the precise moment of New Year, they write it on the screen and hold it there. In fact, that's what I did, but afterwards I deleted it, because when the writing appears the audience might think that it's the beginning of the credits and get up and leave and so miss the freeze frame at the end of the film.

ME: In its present state, though, I still think that's too much, when the balloon seller stands up. Every time I've seen the film I've thought to myself that it should end with the boy sitting down.

JP: I thought about that, too, but when he stands up he gives this good, touching stare, and I didn't want to give that up. I felt that the way he looks is worth a lot and that the film should end that way. As for the shot where he's sitting down, in the lab I worked on that and edited it so that it is repeated several times, thus dragging out the shot.

ME: The end of the film is its most brilliant part. But I thought it would have been better for the film to end with a fade to black, rather than with that freeze frame. Although the music we hear at the end there provides an interesting contrast with the image.

JP: I don't know, perhaps. I thought that it should move. I didn't want to end it with a fade to black. I don't know what the reason is. It's more to do with feeling than logic.

ME: Having said that, my suggestion would have made the ending of the film more bitter.

HG: It would have provoked a feeling of mixed sweetness and bitterness, which wouldn't have been a bad thing at all for the film. The sweetness of Razieh and her brother getting what they wanted, mixed with the bitterness of the Afghan boy left all alone.

JP: No, I didn't want it to be that bitter. Although I don't have a reason for that.

HG: Many people have wondered about the father's second job, about the cotton carding. So tell us, who did that polishing kit belong to?

JP: It belonged to the house. It wasn't for anyone's job.

ME: But it was a professional kit!

HG: It didn't look like they were the kind of fancy people that would spend all their time polishing and thus need such a professional kit.

JP: A lot of houses have a box of polishing equipment.

HG: Yes, but a box, not a professional kit.

ME: The city council and the traffic police should be happy with the "anti-moped" bit of the film!

JP: Before the guy on the moped passes Razieh and the Armenian woman on the sidewalk, causing Razieh to drop the 500-toman note that falls through the grating on the street, we'd already set up that moment earlier in the film. In the scene where the porters are carrying the mirrors and candlesticks, three or four motorcyclists pass by.

ME: It all feels predestined.

JP: I felt that if it had been only that one moped that came along in that scene and led to the money falling, it would have been too little. A moped passes in front of the pastry shop, too. I worked to get the sound to repeat and make it more intense so that a background would be created in the viewer's mind. Even before the guy on the moped causes her to drop the money, he almost hits several other people, the better to show his indifference and couldn't-care-less attitude. And the girl—that's my own daughter!

HG: The scenes where they squabble when they're trying to get the money back from under the grating reminded me of the film *The Key*.[8] Were you thinking of that when you were filming those scenes?

JP: I don't remember whether I was thinking of *The Key* then or not. The truth is that I wasn't thinking about any other film. I was thinking that the efforts to get the money back had turned into a children's game and that it wasn't really important anymore whether they got it back or not. And when the shop owner comes, the smile is wiped from their faces because the game is over. For the Afghan boy in particular, everything is over. Of course, out of this squabbling and back-and-forth there came excitement, but more than that, what was important about that game for me, more than it creating excitement, was that the children had lost hope, and their efforts turned into a game that was completely childish.

ME: Tell us about knocking down the kitchen wall.
JP: We shot two scenes in Kashan, the first one in the little bazaar, and two shots where we are entering the house and see the girl coming out. To get these shots, I either had to pan out with the camera, which I didn't want to do, or use a 35mm lens, in which case the image would have been distorted. So we ended up having to knock down the kitchen wall of one of the houses so we could shoot using a 50mm lens. When the crew saw I had a wall knocked down so I could use a different lens, they realized how serious we were!

ME: In that same shot, there is a hand rolling up a carpet in the corner of the frame.
JP: I think it gives the shot a dynamic character, and it also shows us that *Nowruz* is fast approaching.[9]

HG: You're now heading off to the Turin Film Festival. How do you think the film will be received there?
JP: At the Tokyo International Film Festival I met a woman and man who loved the film and were talking about it obsessively. Afterwards I found out that the man was one of the judges for Turin. In Locarno, too, Baran Kowsari—Rakhshan Bani-Etemad's daughter—insisted that her mother, who is also a Turin judge, would vote for *The White Balloon*. So we know that we've already got two votes, and in fact Alberto Barbera, the head of the judging committee in Turin, was also a judge for Cannes' Caméra d'Or award and is a supporter of our film.

ME: Has the film had a public screening anywhere?
JP: When I go to Turin I'll go to Paris, too, because the film is having a public screening there as part of a four-day program showing all the winners of the Caméra d'Or. There are seventeen films, and *The White Balloon* is the opening film. After that it'll be shown at the Belfort Festival.

ME: What about a public screening in the US?
JP: I think that'll happen in January, which will be good publicity for the Oscars. The film's distributor, October Films, is very hopeful it will be one of the five

nominees. They told me that last year the distributor of *Through the Olive Trees*, CiBy 2000, made a mess of its chances, because it had three films that had made a lot of money and for tax reasons, to avoid heavy taxes, it chose to sacrifice *Through the Olive Trees* and screened it only in distant and thinly populated places. But our distributor told us that they are a small distributor and therefore our film is their best chance, meaning that they're going to focus all their efforts on it and not squander this opportunity.

ME: How was the film received at the New York festival?[10]
JP: I wasn't at the screening. I made it to the press conference, but it was scheduled at exactly the same time as the verdict was due to be announced at the O. J. Simpson trial, and that's all anyone in America wanted to talk about that day. Despite all that, lots of people came to the press conference and the reactions were all positive. Jamsheed Akrami showed it to his doctoral students at the university there and I was able to go to the screening and participate in the discussion about it. He also mentioned the name of a cinema there—I don't remember it just now— and said that if the film were to be screened there, it would do well and promote itself. I had met the owner of that cinema in Cannes, and in fact he had been competing with October Films to buy the rights to *The White Balloon*. He told me that he had wanted to buy the film on account of his daughter, because Razieh's moods and the way she behaved reminded him of her. He praised the film and said that I'd discovered a new Shirley Temple. In American cinema it's rare to see young girls; usually when there are adolescents or children in American films, they are boys.

Notes

1. Azerbaijani Turks who speak a Turkic language. Jafar Panahi himself is Azeri.
2. From the Caspian port city of Rasht.
3. Although Iran has not ratified international conventions that regulate the minimum age for labor, a child may not legally work in Iran until the age of fifteen. There are loopholes, however, that make this law easy to circumvent.
4. A dish of fried lamb or goat organ meat.
5. March 21, 1994.
6. In the Gregorian calendar, this corresponds to the period from March 21, 1995 to March 20, 1996.
7. Because *Nowruz*, the Iranian New Year celebration, marks the spring equinox, it has a precise starting time at which families gather, often listening to the radio or watching television for the exact moment, known as *sāl-tahvil* ("delivery of the year"). It is this that Jafar Panahi is referring to here.

8. *The Key* [*Kelid*] (Ebrahim Forouzesh, 1987), also written by Abbas Kiarostami.

9. This indicates that the carpet has been cleaned. Spring cleaning is a traditional part of the *Nowruz* season.

10. The 1995 New York Film Festival.

Jafar Panahi[1]

Liza Béar / 1996

From *Bomb,* No. 55 (Spring 1996): 10, 12–13. This interview was commissioned by and first published in BOMB Magazine, from BOMB 55/Spring 1996 © Bomb Magazine, New Art Publications, and its Contributors. All rights reserved. The BOMB Digital Archive can be viewed at https://bombmagazine.org.

An exquisitely crafted debut feature, Jafar Panahi's *The White Balloon* is a compelling tribute to the aesthetic merits of simplicity. A little girl wants to buy a special fish for the New Year's celebrations: to get to it, she must forge her way through a sly, treacherous world of adults in the back streets and alleyways of Tehran. The film so imaginatively inhabits the macro mindset of a seven-year-old, for whom the tiniest setback is a momentous hurdle as to bring high drama and a delicious humor to every step of her single-minded journey. Under Panahi's impeccable direction, Aida Mohammadkhani plays her role with grave charm and unflinching determination.

A Cannes 1995 Caméra d'Or winner, *The White Balloon* is also a salute to the strong collaborative tradition of Iranian filmmaking that has emerged in the wake of that country's devastating social upheavals. By the time I saw *The White Balloon* at the Montreal Film Festival, the story of the making of the film was already legendary. As it goes, Panahi told Abbas Kiarostami his idea for the scenario while working as Kiarostami's assistant director on *Through the Olive Trees.* Kiarostami not only encouraged him to make the film but offered to "write" the script for it by narrating the story into a tape recorder as they drove from one location to another.

Liza Béar: Was there a ban on the showing of Western films in Iran when you were growing up?

Translator: I can answer for him. Only after the 1979 revolution, and at that point he was already eighteen years old. Do you still want me to translate the question?

LB: Well, yes. I want to know what films he was seeing.

Jafar Panahi: I used to go to the movies from the age of twelve, but I never took them seriously. I never thought of myself as a filmmaker or of becoming a film-maker. I became much more serious after the revolution and I started to study a number of filmmakers on video because their movies were not available in the theaters.

LB: You mentioned *The Bicycle Thieves* by Vittorio De Sica at the New York Film Festival press conference. Were there any others?

JP: At different periods I liked different filmmakers, but then I discovered our own cinema, Iranians who made films before I did, and they were the strongest influences on me.

LB: Did the absence of genre films, of Western commercial cinema on Iranian screens, mean that Iranian filmmakers were able to draw on their own first-hand experience in imagining a scenario, rather than making comments on other films?

JP: I appreciate the observation. Yes, obviously I paid a lot of attention to local detail in my film. Beyond what you see on the screen, I can't really elaborate on anything except that the joy of a conversation like this for me would be to find out if my audience has also noticed all those details.

LB: Uh huh. Do little girls in Iran always get their own way?

JP: [laughter] Probably as much as anywhere else in the world!

LB: Especially when they're so persistent. The red bill that Razieh, the seven-year-old girl in your film, loses says 5000 on it. How much is that worth?

JP: It's equivalent to 500 tomans. It's worth $1.50. But that's one third of a day's pay for that family.

LB: As well as coming up with the initial story idea and directing *The White Balloon*, you were responsible for the art direction, you built the set, and you edited the film. How did you manage all these roles?

JP: For two reasons. We couldn't have a very large crew for this film. One was the (small) scale of the production and the size of the budget: We just couldn't afford to. The other, just as important, was the presence of a kid. The more people you have on the set, the more the kid may be bothered by their presence. For instance, I never use a script supervisor. I take care of continuity myself. Also, I don't have anyone clap the slate because that is disturbing for the child. I wanted the child very naturally to flow into the part without somebody shouting, "Now we're ready!"

LB: You got the locations to match perfectly, which was very important for a film that takes place in real time.

JP: It's very hard to get that kind of match. I spent an incredible amount of time doing it. For example: the little girl's house is in Tehran, but when she opens the door onto an alley, that's another town. I know the kind of passageway that that kind of a house should be a part of. In a sense, I created my own architecture by putting different places together. The tailor's shop was a real shop but not in Tehran, somewhere else. The snake charmers were in Tehran but at quite a distance from the house. No two locations that you see as adjacent in the film are in close proximity to one another in real life.

LB: How did the story elements come together?

JP: A school friend of mine, Parviz Shahbazi, and I had an idea for a short film. I have two children, a thirteen-year-old son and seven-year-old girl, the same age as Razieh in the film. My premise for the short film was very simple: a little girl wants to make a special fish for the New Year. All the other characters and situations in the feature-length version were added by Abbas Kiarostami, except for the old lady who helps Razieh find the money; she was part of the original concept.

LB: What ethnic groups were represented in the film?

JP: The old lady was part of the Polish emigration that took place during the Second World War. The tailor is from the Turkish minority. The fish vendor is from a city in northern Iran that is on the Caspian Sea and has its own dialect. And the soldier is from another part of the country altogether.

LB: Did you have to travel a lot during the casting to find exactly the right actors?

JP: To some extent I did travel, but in many instances I got extremely lucky. The very first day of casting we found the lead character, Razieh. We had scheduled to go to two different classes with a video camera and do a test of several girls, but when we went into our very first classroom, there she was.

LB: She'd never acted before, right?

JP: If she'd had the slightest bit of experience I wouldn't have cast her. Sometimes in five frames you can tell whether the person is right for the part. You can spend hours and days looking around, but sometimes there's a particular moment when your eyes connect and you think, this is it. That's what happened to me with Aida.

LB: Did anyone in the film have acting experience?

JP: The only character who had a smattering of film experience, although she's not really considered a professional actress, was Razieh's mother. She was the subject of a documentary on her life by another Iranian filmmaker. In fact, she's married to a friend of mine who made a very good movie called *The Fish*,[2] which went to a lot of film festivals. But to give you an idea of how much she knew about filmmaking, on the last day of my work with her she asked me whether I was also a cameraman like the documentary director.

LB: You could take it as a compliment that she didn't feel intimidated by you as a director.
JP: I agree that the less the actors are intimidated by the director, the better it is for the film. It enriches the process of filmmaking as a collective experience, and as far as I'm concerned if the actors don't see other movies at all, I would like that even better, complete purity as far as exposure to cinema.

LB: What was your own childhood like growing up in Tehran?
JP: I grew up in the same environment, in the maze of back alleys that you see in *The White Balloon*, with the same kind of family, a family that was struggling to survive. My father was a house painter.

LB: Did he have a second job, like the unseen father in the script?
JP: No, but he was really a film buff, crazy about going to the movies. I used to go to work with him when I wasn't going to school in the summer or during the holidays. My father didn't like me to see the movies that he was seeing. But I was just as interested in going to the movies as he was, and since he wouldn't take me I went on my own. Sometimes he would put me in charge of the workers on a contract job. He'd say, "I have to do something, I'll be right back." I was about twelve years old at the time. When he didn't come back after half an hour I realized that he must have gone to see a movie. Once I'd figured that out, I would also abandon the workers and go to see a movie. I usually tried to see a different one, but sometimes it might happen that I ended up going to the same movie as my father. If he found out, there would be punishment later at home and he would promise never to go to the movies again.

LB: Sounds like the beginning of a good scenario.
JP: I used to complain: How come you go to see them, but you tell me that they are not good for me?

LB: Just like the little girl in the film!
JP: Yes, when she's told not to stop at the snake charmers and she does. But now, as it turns out, my own son is totally in love with American action-adventure movies. They're only available on lousy-quality video cassettes on the black market.

And I keep telling him, don't watch them. I try to keep him from seeing those kinds of movies, just as my father tried to stop me. And my son's response is exactly like mine: I just want to find out why you think this is no good for me.

LB: Did you go to film school immediately after high school?

JP: When I graduated from high school the Iranian Revolution broke out and the colleges closed for a long time, two or three years. I had to look for other things to do, including going to the front and taking still photographs. And after a while, when I had made some contacts there, I asked them to give me a 16mm film camera so I could shoot a documentary. This was the Iran-Iraq War. The front was in the southern part of Iran.

LB: Did you see action? Were you involved in the combat?

JP: Yes, I was conscripted.

LB: It must have been great training for the eye, aside from everything else.

JP: The war documentaries were very encouraging to me because I realized I was doing film work. After the war was over I came back—there's a college entrance examination in Iran that is very important, so that was incentive for me to work really hard to prepare for it. It's like the French baccalauréate. The first year in film school we weren't required to specialize, but my first love as a filmmaker was editing. I would get my hands on any surplus footage or reels that I could, just to put something together. Sometimes I would beg my friends to let me edit their projects for them. And once I had done some work as an editor, I really felt that I should be making my own films. So I became one of seven students—out of sixty—accepted by the film school that year, to be trained and graduate as a director.

LB: That's a pretty selective system compared to the US film schools. How many films have you made altogether?

JP: Three short documentaries and two short dramatic films, which won awards in a number of domestic film festivals.

LB: Did you travel anywhere other than to the front, which is not exactly traveling?

JP: My very first foreign trip in my entire life was to France to participate in the Cannes Film Festival this year.

LB: Maybe because you were all working on home turf, the dialogue in *The White Balloon* sounds particularly lively and authentic. For instance, that very suspenseful sequence with the snake charmers, and later the bickering between the tailor and his client.

JP: I wanted to capture day-to-day life in Tehran, but also the script set up strong situations that allowed the characters to engage in disputatious dialogue. It was important to me that the characters each represent a different segment of the population, a particular mindset. It's through the dialogue that they reveal their unique characters.

LB: Was any of the dialogue improvised?

JP: Because of our style of working with the actors, we only used improvisation. We never gave them a script. We would just explain a situation to them and talk about it. We would say: In this situation you have to express such and such a feeling and this is your goal. You put it into your own words. We might also say a few words to get them going, but that's it. This is the beauty of working with non-professionals, compared to a professional actor who would say, I want my lines, I can't work any other way.

LB: So your background in documentary must have contributed to this way of working.

JP: Not only is the documentary approach very helpful in terms of creating dialogue and improvisation, but it's also very helpful when it comes to découpage. It almost forces you to be spontaneous. No matter how carefully you create a certain découpage in your mind, you still have to make changes due to the abilities or lack of abilities of your actors. In a situation like this I think it's an advantage if you edit your own films. It's amazing—not only was our cast nonprofessional but so was the crew. It was my first feature film, my cameraman's first film, my soundman's first film. It was a debut for everybody.

LB: You shot in 35mm.

JP: An Arriflex. We used three kinds of tripods including the high hat because there were so many low-angle shots. We mostly shot the film in natural light, and even when using reflectors we had to be very careful. I didn't want anything too imposing like a huge reflector. There were only a couple of instances where we really had to light the scene, like inside the tailor's shop. I was very careful to pick locations which most of the day were in shadow so we wouldn't have to deal with variations in sunlight.

LB: I understand the use of the goldfish in the New Year's ceremony is not part of the Islamic tradition, but goes back to an older Persian tradition that predates Islam and that some Iranians have fought to preserve.

JP: I'm not sure exactly at what point in time the fish became part of the New Year's Eve ritual, but in terms of what it means, it's a dynamic symbol of life.

LB: What are the seven "Sins" or elements associated with the ceremony?

JP: We have a letter "Sin" which is like "S" for Sally in our language. The seven elements start with a "Sin," but the fish isn't one of them. The fish was added, as was the mirror. The other elements are a coin, garlic, flour, a dried fruit not found in the US, and a rice dish. Some people believe that if they have the first five or six elements together, for the last one or two they can improvise. I forgot one, *sabze,* which means grass. *Sabze* represents green things, spring, the sense of new life.

LB: What was the special award you won in Tokyo?

JP: I won the best first film award, shared with the US film *The Usual Suspects. The White Balloon* also won an award called The Flying Dragon, which is given by the Mayor of Tokyo for the best film of the festival. Obviously I'm very happy about it, not only because I'd just lost all my money in Tokyo, just like Razieh in the film, but because the amount of the award, $160,000, will enable me to produce my next two films. They'll also both be stories about children, one will take place almost entirely in Tehran and the other in Iran, but outside of Tehran.

LB: Well, I hope you haven't lost any money in New York.

JP: No, not yet!

Notes

1. This interview was conducted with the invaluable help of a Farsi interpreter while Mr. Panahi was in town for the screening of his film at the New York Film Festival.
2. This is Kambuzia Partovi's 1991 film, of which Panahi was assistant director.

An Interview with Jafar Panahi:
Honest to God, He Is Not a Copycat

Ahmad Talebinejad / 1997

From *Film International* (Tehran) 5.2 (August 1, 1997): 42–47.

Ahmad Talebinejad: You are one of the most exceptional filmmakers in Iran in the sense that your only two feature films have been awarded the grand prizes of the Cannes, Locarno, and other noteworthy festivals.

Jafar Panahi: Honestly, when they informed me that I had won the Caméra d'Or for *The White Balloon*, I didn't realize what had happened, but I accepted it in quite a relaxed manner. Ali-Reza Shoja-Nouri, the state official accompanying me, said, "Don't be anxious when you go up there." I was not anxious at all; when I got up on the stage to say a few sentences, I felt relaxed. Shoja-Nouri himself translated my speech in a rather quavering voice because he believed something important had transpired. I felt that I had passed a crucial point in my career. Now the stakes were higher and everyone asked me about my next film. Then I realized what a complicated journey I was about to embark upon. Some people advised me against making my second film in the near future, but I didn't take the matter too seriously. Because I was gaining experience, I wasn't frightened; I began my second film under the same circumstances in which I had made the first one.

AT: Aren't you worried about the future? Everyone expects so much more of you. History shows that those filmmakers who achieve great success in their first or second film have a difficult path ahead since the conditions are not always conducive to their desire. Orson Welles, John Huston, or even the Algerian director Mohamma Lakhadar Hamina (who was dismissed after he won the Palme d'Or) are well-known cases. Anyway, you have a bumpy road in front of you.

JP: We have always lived under exceptional conditions. In the Iranian movie industry, a filmmaker consumes only ten percent of his energy on directing a film. The rest is wasted on marginal affairs, from the never-ending conflicts with the censors to tracking down the necessary equipment. When I wanted to select the cast for *The Mirror* from among the students at a school, I was forbidden from even entering the school because I was accused of propagating Christianity in *The White Balloon*—one of the good characters in that film was an elderly Christian lady. Moreover, the Ministry of Education forbade showing the film to students. Finally, I got permission for my assistant to enter the school.

Anyhow, it was possible to find another way, is the point. The Iranian film industry has proved that filmmakers must be thick-skinned people if they wish to achieve their goals, so I'm not worried about the hard times ahead of me. The real dilemma occurs when you are forced to surrender to the imposed situation. There are those filmmakers among us who haven't surrendered to such situations, and they haven't made any films for seven years. Of course, there have been others who have made their films under unbearable circumstances. I know now that people expect more from me than before, and if I produce a film of a lesser quality than *The White Balloon*, they won't accept it. Yes, I believe that Orson Welles worked even harder after he made *Citizen Kane* because that film prompted a greater expectation from him. When I began *The Mirror*, I was aware of the consequences. I even thought that the critics might not appreciate it, but I believed in the film and I felt I had to make it. During the shooting of the film, I had a feeling that it would be better than *The White Balloon* because I was applying the practical experience I had gained. And I can only hope for the same in my next film.

AT: Now there is a second problem. There are doubts about you. The general conception is that you are another Kiarostami, and you have to try doubly hard when you come up against this idea. That is to say, you now have to somehow extricate yourself from Kiarostami's shadow.

JP: In the history of cinema, no two great filmmakers have been alike, and their greatness lies in the very soul of their character. As for myself, I believe that other filmmakers have been in a similar situation. For example, Bergman's assistant made a film that also carried Bergman's name. Well, I turned Kiarostami's script into *The White Balloon,* and I was also his assistant in the past. Young filmmakers have long been influenced by directors before them, and you could label it influence or imitation. I must establish my own identity and have my works judged in relation to the films that preceded mine. And yet I am not afraid of being accused of being influenced by such and such a filmmaker. I'm of two minds about this, as you can see.

AT: You are amongst the filmmakers who have been favored by luck and fate. As I recall, before making *The White Balloon*, you were supposed to make a film titled *The Little Locomotive Driver* for a commercial producer. You waited a year and eventually aborted the project. I believe if you had made that film, you wouldn't have made *The White Balloon* or *The Mirror*. I say this because many young filmmakers have directed their debuts for such producers and then continued on that same path for the rest of their careers.

JP: Before making *The White Balloon*, I made two shorts, *The Friend* and *The Final Exam*. I gained experience through them, and in *The Friend* I emphasized the acting. After graduating from college, I went to work in the Radio and TV Center in Bandar Abbas, and there I continued the practice of using child actors as in *The Friend*. In my second film I focused on découpage. When I returned to Tehran I hastened to make a professional feature film. After watching many Iranian films over and over again, I realized my potential was no less than the directors of those films. I just wanted to make my own film, by hook or by crook, so I called on the producer you mentioned. After I began shooting, I found it an unsatisfactory project and I decided to stop. But when I started *The White Balloon,* I asked a nonprofessional producer to make it because I didn't want them to interfere in the making of the film. I was lucky enough to pick the best crew possible. If I had used a professional cinematographer instead of Farzad Jadat, the outcome would not have been the same.

AT: It is a given in this world that one must use a professional crew in order to make a good film; the opposite occurs in Iranian cinema. I think that even Kiarostami makes his films in an amateurish way, meaning the director has to do everything by himself. I don't know if the situation is the same for other directors in the world.

JP: When I told the foreign reporters and filmmakers about the circumstances in which we make our films, they were surprised. You know, when you work with amateurs, they try to display their best. In France we visited a location at which they were shooting a scene of a French film. There were at least ten "cinemobiles" there, while we don't even have one of them, and we don't need them. To make *The Mirror,* I had a crew of six, and I didn't need an inefficient seventh.

AT: Can this be a kind of inspiration for other independent filmmakers around the world?

JP: I don't think so. For example, we shot *The Mirror* in the traffic jams of Tehran, and we did it without incident. But if you do the same thing in Europe, you have to ask for the drivers' permission one by one.

AT: I think independent filmmakers in any country would work in similar conditions if they were forced to, because they want to make their films.

JP: I was offered the opportunity to make films abroad, but I declined for two clear reasons: First, I don't know foreigners very well, and secondly, I am familiar with my own culture and nation. In any case, one can make a low-budget film in any country, but one has to apply different approaches. Low-budget filmmaking has no specific formula, and one's approach is not applicable in all countries.

AT: Nevertheless, the director plays a more important role in this type of film-making, and it is the filmmaker, above all, who must shoulder any problems due to these nonprofessionals.

JP: But don't forget that every filmmaker considers the risk of low box-office returns. As for *The White Balloon,* I had a state producer backing me, so I wasn't too worried about it.

AT: Did the professional producers contact you after your international success? I'm sure you know that winning awards at the festivals is not so important to them and they think only of the box-office returns.

JP: Naturally many of them did, and they knew that they would have to accept my criteria. Now that I was successful, I didn't have to agree with everything they offered. Anyhow, there are lots of proposals that are never put into action.

AT: In the Iranian cinema, the situation is like the opposing poles of a magnet. If the filmmaker achieves cultural success, then the producers run away from him because they think this guy can't double their investment.

JP: It was completely the opposite in regard to *The White Balloon.* Besides winning some prizes, the revenue from the international distribution brought back some twenty times more than the invested budget.

AT: Well, that's a kind of random occurrence, because a film might not win any prizes and no distributor will buy it. The Iranian producers think more about the domestic market. Okay, what's your opinion about cinema? You revealed your interest in Kiarostami in your very first short film, *The Friend,* which is influenced by Kiarostami's *The Bread and Alley.*

JP: I like *The Bread and Alley* so much that I wrote a sketch based upon it, and I even emphasized its influence on *The Friend* in the scene where the little boy is shown in front of a theater showing Kiarostami's earlier films.

AT: In *The Final Exam*, you worked more on the rhythm. I think the rhythm of the film, which depicts two teenage girls, one from northern Iran and the other from the south, is influenced by the rhythm of southern Iranian music.

JP: I shot a sequence of this film for the professional producers to show them that I could make a proper feature film. In the scene a little girl dreams and, yes, the musical rhythms serve an important purpose.

AT: Southern Iranian music is influenced by African music, which has an appealing fast rhythm. I think you based the découpage of the film on that kind of music.

JP: By making this film, I wanted to have something in hand as a sample for producers. And because of that, I focused carefully on each element.

AT: Now let's turn to *The White Balloon*. The little girl is under great pressure from the opening scene of the film until the end—she is almost always crying. This is completely acceptable as far as reality is concerned, since many Iranian children (especially those from working-class families) live in such conditions. I think that a considerable portion of the film's success is due to the girl's frightened, tearful face. For example, in the snake-charmers sequence, she is really tortured. Incidentally, if this sequence had been edited out, it wouldn't have harmed the film, because nothing important happens in this scene.

JP: Let's go back to the time period before production. When I started, I didn't think of anything but making my film. I didn't think of the festivals because I knew nothing about them; I didn't expect anything. I was given the opportunity to make a film and it was the only thing important to me. I remember during the final days of shooting, I read in the newspaper that *The White Balloon* would be featured in the Children Film Festival in Isfahan. We were so pleased, and this meant that we had to complete the film. You see, even Isfahan surprised me. Now, if you say the sequence with the snake charmers is redundant, you may want to take out other sequences and see that nothing happens to the film. The film is not supposed to be dramatic at all, but basically creates an atmosphere. In other words, we wanted to film a real picture of the ongoing situations. The atmosphere and the relationships were the most important things.

AT: You are not a documentary filmmaker, then why did you emphasize so strongly the documentary aspects of the film?

JP: The kind of film we make is something between documentary and feature films.

AT: Kiarostami's films are also like that, or, say, Makhmalbaf's *Gabbeh* and *Salaam Cinema*.

JP: Yes, and because these films are so in touch with reality, they resemble documentaries. One scene in *The Mirror* shows the little girl in an emotional state, and she refuses to act anymore. At the Locarno Festival, many people asked me if I had reconciled with the girl. They thought it really happened. When I explained to them that it was just a scripted performance in the film, they didn't believe me, probably because they expected the sequence to be shot in just one day. This is a new style of documentary, and it cannot be separated from reality. This tendency towards such a cinema reveals my intentions about documentary.

AT: Well, what is the artistic function of this documentary-like film? Flaherty also worked in this way—I mean, he used the matters of reality in dramatic ways.

JP: We must first consider this point: What is our concept of cinema? In my opinion, if the filmmaker is honest enough toward his audience and is respectful of their intelligence, he will not insult them with clichés. He has to find his own method. One of these methods is to use reality—a fresh look at the very reality that the spectator encounters in everyday events. In *The Mirror*, the primary motif is the criticism of social mores. We live in a world in which people show off, but they still don't believe in their own words. This was the main theme of the film.

AT: Is this why you named it *The Mirror*?

JP: Yes. The film intends to reflect the realities. In the sequence where the girl rebels, she is in fact protesting against the other actors because she is a witness to their pretending. Then we follow her with a candid camera, and we see two different realities—a real image and a figurative image of reality. And they are not too distant from each other. This could be considered as a type of style, but I don't mind that. You know, I'm experimenting. Structuralist art critics believe that the structure of every work of art is influenced by the social surroundings. Thus it is natural that films with social themes should have seemingly simple and documentary-like structures. If you have seen most of the notable Iranian films, even the pre-revolution ones, you will notice they are constructed in this way— meaning that we are always suffering from the big social problems.

AT: Yes, we see this kind of structure in the works of Sohrab Shahid-Saless, too. In fact, those distinguished Iranian filmmakers have been able to develop a new form of documentary filmmaking.

JP: I daresay, if someday I ask professionals to act in my films, I'll expect them to forget about the usual routines and to act as "normal" people. They will have to "do as the Romans do" when working with my crew.

AT: Now, why are children always the heroes of your films?

JP: As you know, the best Iranian movies are those about children. This is also a result of the social conditions. I mean, when you're not able to express your words through adults because of censorship, you transfer them to children and speak through their language. There may come a day when social conditions change and Iranian filmmakers do not have to choose the children's language and world. There are too many Iranian films about children, while there are hardly any *for* children. Unfortunately there has been no other choice. I admit to the fact that the children have been our pretext.

AT: If you were asked to make a film for children—say, a fantasy—would you do it? Do you have a good imagination?

JP: That depends on the subject. I had a painful childhood, and I always believed that the adults were responsible. Yet I have always kept reality as my haven instead of imagination. My teenage son is interested in action sci-fi, but when I was his age I loved *The Bread and Alley*. Some years ago, when I was having severe financial difficulties, I was asked to direct a number of commercial TV shows. I agreed, but the following morning when I got up to go to work, I felt feverish and fell sick. Now, if you don't take it as a proud boast, I can say that I am capable of making sci-fi, fantasy, and commercial movies as well. Every filmmaker has such potential, but it is his scruples that must steer him away from vulgarity. It's our conscience that reminds us not to compromise our vision and not to resort to that kind of filmmaking.

AT: The other impediment is one's feeling of shame when harshly judged by critics and the intelligentsia.

JP: Most of all, I would feel ashamed of myself if I were to make a compromised film. I can compensate the critics and the intelligentsia by making the next film, but I can't solve the problem of a high fever!

AT: If you couldn't make films like *The White Balloon* or *The Mirror* because of what we might call "conditions," then would you yield to the producers and their orders, or would you rather not make any more films?

JP: I don't know. It depends on the circumstances, but I'm sure I can't forget about the fever!

AT: Now that you are a renowned filmmaker in the world, how do you think Iranian cinema can compete with world cinema?

JP: It was cheerful news that *The White Balloon* has been a hit in some countries. That means that many people have gone to see the film. I myself, plus the other Iranian filmmakers, wish we could find a way into the international market. The success at the festivals is periodic, and one comes to the end of his career sooner or later. We have to find a way to get into the world's theaters, but that depends on Iran's cinema policy. When I hear the comments of spectators at the festivals, I find them refreshing and it makes me happy that these films are not being neglected as they are in Iran. But I remind myself, festival attendees are often cinephiles; what about the common movie-goers? Do they understand the films as well and get as much pleasure?

AT: But the public screenings of *The White Balloon* and *Gabbeh* in American and European theaters have been successful.

JP: An American commentator remarked that if we consider the total expense of *The White Balloon*, we find it one of the real hits of the year, even though it was ranked among the failures in America. In the US a movie is exhibited in at least one hundred theaters, but here *The White Balloon* had only two showings. We must have more of them.

AT: But movies like Jim Jarmusch's are not shown in one hundred theaters.

JP: I know we can't do as well as Spielberg's films do. Maybe we will find a formula someday in the future.

AT: Let me point out that if your films, Kiarostami's, Makhmalbaf's, or others' works can establish a kind of cultural dialogue between us and the "Westerners," then we have achieved the intended success. Since we have always been over-exposed to their films, it would be a great success if an American TV network aired an Iranian film. In other words, these films could function as our language.

JP: Well, that is also short-lived, and we have to find a way to continue.

AT: In your opinion, what is interesting in our cinema that attracts Western viewers?

JP: In two words: sincerity and frankness.

AT: You mean, these are inherent to our films and not so much to others?

JP: Sincerity runs in our films. Of course, some Western filmmakers are sincere, too, but we hardly ever see it in their films. Our cinema says that humane and lovely moments can be created through simple matters. This causes the foreign spectator to acquire the power to discover these ideas and to get pleasure from this cathartic discovery. This is contrary to commercial cinema around the world, which subjugates the spectator and deprives them of this discovery.

AT: Turning back to *The Mirror*, it has been quite controversial. First, the film hasn't been shown in Iran yet, and it is to be released at Fajr Film Festival in mid-winter. Considering the film's synopsis and other comments about it, we can conclude that the film is a highly metaphorical one.

JP: The fact is that Iranian cinema has suffered from severe conditions within the last two to five years, and it is possible that this film was a reaction against the restrictions. I'm very happy, in spite of the problems, that I could make the film I wanted to make.

AT: You have said that *The White Balloon* is a kind of dry run in comparison to *The Mirror*. Why do you feel this way?

JP: Every film is in a way a dry run to its sequel. In *The White Balloon*, I didn't know what the reaction would be to what I was doing, but in *The Mirror* I worked more consciously. And one likes best his newest film that has been made more knowingly. If I make my next film under better conditions, I may call *The Mirror* a dry run, too. *The Mirror* expresses the same words I wanted to say, and I'm happy about it. I made *The White Balloon* because I felt it was getting too late for me to make my film; but I made *The Mirror* because I felt it was the word of the world and it had to be said.

AT: One can guess that you took into consideration the taste of the directors and the festival juries when you were making *The Mirror*. This concern for the metaphorical aspects reveals your knowledge about the festivals. An example is when the little girl in *The Mirror* complains about wearing her scarf and takes it off.

JP: I won't deny this issue concerning the festivals. I knew about them, and I believed they were saturated with films whose heroes were children; I felt that I could pour out my thoughts only through this channel. Then I forgot about them and I tried to think about the film itself; I made what I wanted to make. If I only cared for their tastes, then I couldn't make any more children's films. Even Marco Muller, the director of the Locarno Festival, told me, "When I heard that you were making another film with children, I thought you were wrong to do so. But when I watched the film, I changed my opinion." I intentionally applied the technique of "a film within a film," even though many others had recently used this clichéd technique. Of course, the subject and content required it anyway. In this sense I included some elements that put me at a disadvantage at the festivals. I decided to make this film under conditions very similar to McCarthyism in order to prevent my fever from returning!

AT: What is your next film?

JP: I don't know. I have some sketches, but I don't know which one will work.

AT: Will you produce your next film under the same conditions?

JP: I don't know. It depends on when we start shooting. Another characteristic of Iranian cinema is that no film is defined when it's in pre-production. It is not even a complete film until the time of public screening. This applied to the making of *The Mirror*. While auditioning thousands of female students, I picked one of them who appeared to be a better choice than the others. In the beginning, everything went well, and she acted for the first day. In the opening scene, she remains facing the camera after the other children leave. In the next shot, I asked her to show sadness. After multiple takes, I realized that she couldn't do it. So I asked Aida Mohammadkhani's[1] younger sister to play the part, because I knew her beforehand. But I wasn't satisfied with her voice. Now that it's done, I'm pretty satisfied with her.

AT: Aida acted in a couple of other films, and they were rather unsatisfactory.

JP: OK, we can discuss child actors or so-called non-actors. In my opinion, their position in front of the camera depends on the director of the film. They have pure minds and know nothing about acting. We must put them in front of the camera little by little. You can't treat them like professionals. Sometimes you have to act and ask them to imitate you. In *The White Balloon*, I wanted to see Aida's reaction when she saw me for the first time. In that sequence she began acting her role when she saw us shooting her for the first time. It's part of my job to help these young actors stay in character and act uniformly.

AT: Then this is the reason why those kinds of films are the most "auteurist" films of all—everything depends on the director.

JP: This is not restricted only to acting. You can find that in editing, too. I asked a professional editor to edit *The White Balloon*, and he wanted to cut the long opening scene into pieces. Of course, this would have made my film something different, so I edited it myself. Why don't we use continuity supervisors? The reason is, we do the details by ourselves.

AT: This is due to the amateurish conditions that we discussed earlier. I hope you and a few other good filmmakers in the Iranian cinema remain amateurs forever.

JP: I hope so, too.

Notes

1. The principal girl in *The White Balloon*.

An Interview with Jafar Panahi, Director of *The Mirror*

David Walsh / 1997

From *World Socialist Web Site* (wsws.org), October 6, 1997. Reprinted by permission.

David Walsh: A number of Iranian films have been concerned with the relationship between the filmmaking process and reality. Why do you think this is?

Jafar Panahi: I feel that in order to come across to our audience and in order to develop a good relationship with our audience we must be straightforward and honest with them. So when they see the films they can draw parallels between what they see and the social realities that they face themselves. We respect the audience's intellect. We do not limit them to view things only the way we want them to. We don't limit them like commercial films. We even leave some empty holes in the films for them to develop their own stories. In my opinion today's cinema must respect the audience.

DW: What, in your opinion, is the relationship between realism and poetry?

JP: It is what we are trying to do in cinema. To capture this feeling that evolves within our hearts, without cheating and fraud. And to reflect that in the language of images.

DW: What was the starting point for *The Mirror*?

JP: One time I saw an old woman who was sitting on a bench, with her purse on her lap, looking into space. This image struck me quite strongly. I thought about this woman's life. I thought that she was in a closed circle, and was unable to escape from this circle. This image remained in my mind. And I had the feeling as well that in our society everyone wears a mask over his face, and cannot remove that mask. And I thought that only a child, because he or she has not yet been contaminated, will notice this, and it is only a child who can decide to remove the mask from his or her face, and no longer play a role, and try to be herself.

DW: By what process did you choose this little girl?

JP: We go to schools, we speak with the children. We do some auditions. We ask them questions about themselves, their families. And we ask them to read something out of a book. The child eventually becomes comfortable and starts to show his or her normal behavior. We compare this with the image we have in our own minds of the character. To find the actor for this film I auditioned seven thousand people over a period of about two months. Eventually I decided upon a little girl. She came and acted in the first shot.

In the second shot I told her that she had to act upset. She asked why. I said, because your mother isn't here. She said, well, if my mother doesn't show up, I don't get upset. I said, well, you're playing the role of someone who does get upset when her mother doesn't come for her. She said, well, then go and find someone who does get upset when her mother doesn't show up.

Therefore, from the second shot onward, there is another actor who continues in the film. I was a little undecided about the centerpiece of the film, where the big transition takes place, but when this happened, it convinced me that my decision about the structure of the film was correct.

DW: Don't these performers give more than you expect?

JP: I learn from them. They add things to the film that I realize I hadn't thought of before. And I take those, and I develop them and I give them a new image. That's why our scripts are never very precise. And the film that we end up making is never exactly like the script. This is where our major problem starts. Government officials come and they inspect the film, and they say this is not the same film as the script. "We didn't know before what we wanted to make either."

DW: I assume the girl quitting the film was in the script.

JP: I had thought about that before, but the first little girl confirmed that thought in my mind. And the dialogue that the second girl speaks later on is almost the same as the discussion I had with the first actor. We take impressions from reality and we do not lie to the audience. And we maintain our honesty.

DW: Do you object if we draw much wider social and political implications from the little girl's act?

JP: This is how our films are. There are various levels to our films. There is a surface layer, which is what you see. Based on the perceptive abilities and the viewpoint of the audience to discover and understand the underlying layers of that film. And the more knowledgeable the audience members, the more they will realize the deeper issues underlying the surface. I don't want to limit you to only see the uppermost layer. And I'm hoping that our audiences see that.

No Lies to the Audience

Film Monthly / 2000

From *Film Monthly* (Tehran) 17.248 (2000): 76. Translated by Katayoun Youssefi.

The students leave the school and Bahareh is the only child left alone. She calls home, but no answer. The janitor takes her to the bus stop. She takes the wrong bus, in the opposite direction of her home. She notices her mistake and gets off the bus. While a football match between Iran and South Korea is going on, Bahareh is wandering in the streets.

The Mirror marks the end of Panahi's first stage as a filmmaker. Among Iran's Second-Wave directors, Panahi is one of the first—along with Kiarostami, of course—who stopped making films about children. *The Mirror* was not screened for three years in Iran, at the behest of the director. This is its second public screening after the Children Film Festival in Isfahan. The film was successful outside Iran, though probably not like *The White Balloon*. This interview was conducted during the editing of *The Circle*.

Film Monthly: Some people believe that because of the success of several Iranian films in the international festivals, filmmakers follow the trends of the festivals.
Jafar Panahi: A film that is not good enough, can't find its way through the festivals. First, it should satisfy certain requirements, so that it could receive some publicity. In my case, I had never left the country before *The White Balloon* and knew absolutely nothing about foreign festivals and their culture. When I was making the film I asked myself what I had to say. As someone who has studied cinema, has some experience working as an assistant director, what do I want to say? I was actually testing myself, without thinking about anything else. If we make a film to please someone, we'll most likely ruin it. But we should accept that this type of film gets more attention outside Iran; there is a better understanding of them over there. But I'm not sure if we can say that foreign festivals affect Iranian art films in any way; actually the press should talk about that.

FM: You mean, when a film is accepted in a festival and the filmmaker attends the festival, the atmosphere and discussions around it don't affect the director's work in any way?

JP: After winning the Caméra d'Or at Cannes, I almost stopped reading any reviews or criticism. I didn't want the critics' thoughts to influence me or to direct me towards what they may like. But it is true that a filmmaker's surroundings exert an influence over him in one way or another; he is influenced by his predecessors, for instance. I believe that a successful filmmaker can control all these influences and take advantage of them. They'll always exist, no way to escape them. But it depends on the filmmaker and how he makes use of them consciously in order to improve his work.

FM: Recently, some of the art films have also been successful in Iran. What do you think the reason is? Do you think that *The Circle* or *The Mirror* will attract audiences in the public screenings?

JP: I think Iranian audiences are evolving. Previously their main criterion for going to the cinema was probably the stars. Nowadays people know the name of the filmmakers and they pay attention to that as much as anything. There have been changes in the last ten years in the Iranian cinema, which are not isolated from what has happened outside Iran. When people hear about a film getting a prize in Cannes, they are encouraged to go and watch the film. Maybe they are tired of commercial films and just need a change. We are very happy with these developments. When any of these films enjoy commercial or artistic success, all intellectual filmmakers win. In the past, they showed Iranian films in a few small theatres. Now with this interest in Iranian films, huge movie theatres show them. Anyway, I hope in Iran people will like *The Circle* and *The Mirror*. But unfortunately they show them under poor conditions. *The White Balloon* was never screened in any proper cinema, for instance.

FM: Among the Iranian films in foreign festivals, very few of them are so audacious. Why is that? Why did you work on such a daring subject?

JP: I don't agree with you. The previous films were also audacious, but more subtly. For example, *The Mirror* is talking about a particular situation and a social reality. Pretense is a characteristic of closed societies, and you can see it in the deeper layers of the film. *The Mirror* and *The Circle* each has its own framework. None of them could speak in another framework. On the other hand, I felt that we should make a change in our films; we should go in another direction. We should be honest with the audience and not lie to them. We should take a humanist approach, make a radical transformation, and go beyond merely repeating what's already been done.

An Interview with Jafar Panahi, Director of *The Circle*

David Walsh / 2000

From *World Socialist Web Site* (wsws.org), October 2, 2000. Reprinted by permission.

David Walsh: *The Circle* seems to have an angrier and bolder tone and subject matter than your previous works. Is this the result of the development of the situation in Iran, your own personal development or both?

Jafar Panahi: The truth is that in the previous films, I still tried to show the crucial difficulties, the problems of children. Those films also represented my maturation. They were homework. But the question is: these two children, who tried so hard to achieve what they were after in *The Mirror* and *The White Balloon,* as they grow up, will they keep the same kindness? The actual result is, as we know, that society has them within a circle. And for them to go beyond the boundary of this circle, they will have to pay a certain price. I'm not angry about the situation. The film shows anger in the society, but I'm not angry.

DW: Can you discuss the media and official government response to the film in Iran?

JP: Not too many people have seen the film in Iran. But those who have seen the film, from the intelligentsia, liked it very much. However, when I showed it to a group of members of parliament, they objected to it.

DW: On what basis?

JP: They didn't really specify what part of the film they objected to.

DW: Was there an eight-month hold-up?

JP: I always really try to avoid this subject. I don't really want to think about the two to three years of difficulty that I endured to make this film. It's been very difficult giving birth to this film. But now that the film is being shown, now that the baby is born, I'm enjoying it, and I don't really want to talk about that.

DW: The technique of following one character after another—the circle, *La Ronde*—suggests a process that is pervasive in society that operates as a closed circuit. Was this your intention?
JP: Yes, exactly, and it shows that the characters are trying to get out of the circle also. It's like a relay race. When you're running around the track, and you want to pass the baton to the next. In this film, if one succeeds they all succeed, if one fails, they all fail.

DW: Would an audience in Iran realize before we did that it was a prison hospital in the opening scene?
JP: The new Iranian cinema generally leaves many things up to the viewer, to their knowledge and their thinking, as to how to interpret the film. In this case, some people would realize it very quickly and others wouldn't. It's up to the individual and the knowledge and thinking that they have. This is not specific to Iran. It would be the same everywhere. There are some who would pick things up very quickly.

DW: I meant was there something obviously identifiable?
JP: No, it could have been any kind of hospital.

DW: Nargess says her town is paradise, like the Van Gogh painting. The other woman perhaps knows it is not paradise. Does art present an element in life toward which life must aspire?
JP: In the film, as you see, each new character that's introduced shows a higher degree of experience and a deeper view of life. And so Nargess is very idealistic and not worldly. When she looks at the painting, she doesn't have a real sense of the geography; she just believes it's a beautiful place. Yet the person beside her who is more experienced realizes that that place must have its own problems too.

Art gives hope. Iranian cinema, as well as other forms of art, have been acknowledged internationally and have helped revive national pride and hope.

DW: Is there a progression both in the technique and in the character of the women? Is the final woman a kind of finished product?
JP: There are two ways of looking at this individual. It could be in the first place that she is the sum of all the other characters who've ended up at a dead end. Or she's a person who's accepted the reality, who's acknowledged the truth about society, whereas the other characters are still trying to escape from the circle. So, it depends on how one looks at the character.

DW: Just so there is no misunderstanding—I don't think that the metaphor of the world as a prison is just appropriate for women, or only for Iran. I don't see it as a film merely about Iran, but about conditions everywhere. Such a metaphor does suggest that the world needs to be changed. Would you like us to draw that conclusion?

JP: In my view, everyone in the world lives within a circle, either due to economic, political, cultural, or family problems or traditions. The radius of the circle can be smaller or larger. Regardless of their geographic location, they live within a circle. I hope that if this film has any kind of effect on anyone, it would be to make them try to expand the size of the radius.

DW: While the film treats women, what are the consequences for the men in their lives?

JP: Iranian society, particularly in comparison to this part of the world, is a man's world pretty much. The radius might be marginally larger for men. The purpose of this film was not to be against men or to be a feminist film—it's a film about humanity. Men and women are part of humanity. In the film I never showed any kind of maltreatment or anger from men. For example, we see the women afraid of the police. This may or may not be real. When the police are shown in long shot, they're menacing. However, in medium shot, you can see the policeman has a kind face. And he asks the woman: "Do you need any help?" And also in the scene when the woman was buying a shirt for her fiancé, the storeowner measured it against the soldier's chest. And at the end of the film, when they're in the paddy wagon . . . throughout the film, every single woman wanted to have a smoke. Once they're in the paddy wagon, there is this humanitarian atmosphere.

Joanne Laurier [second interviewer]: Is your point that the army and the police are just made up of ordinary people?

JP: In all my films, you never see an evil character, male or female. I believe everyone is a good person. It could be the result of social difficulties. Even the most dangerous criminal has that sense of humanity. At the bottom he's still a human. It doesn't mean that a criminal shouldn't be punished just because social difficulties have driven him to it. He's guilty because he didn't try to expand the radius of his circle.

DW: This view, which is very rare, is one of the major contributions of the Iranian cinema. Can one sometimes sacrifice a little art in the interest of protest or in the face of injustice? Or is it even a question that arises?

JP: I think this is a little idealistic. History shows many times when artists have sold out to the authorities in order not to show what the social difficulties were.

Or on the other side of the coin, an artist sacrifices himself in order to show what the truth is. And if that happened then it was necessary.

DW: If you want to make a deep impact on people you need art, no?

JP: The impact of art is not instantaneous. If art is extremely successful, then it just touches the society and makes people think about the issues. Art needs people who need art. There is a give and take. There's an exchange. If the society needs the sacrifice of the art and the artist, then that is going to happen.

The Case of Jafar Panahi—An Interview with the Director of *The Circle*

Stephen Teo / 2001

From *Senses of Cinema*, Issue 15, July 18 (July/August), 2001. Reprinted by permission of the author.

Jafar Panahi, born in 1960 in Mianeh, Iran, was ten years old when he wrote his first book, which subsequently won first prize in a literary competition. It was also at that young age that he became familiar with filmmaking: shooting films on 8mm, acting in one 8mm film and assisting in the making of another. Later, he took up photography. On being drafted into the military, Panahi served in the Iran-Iraq War (1980–90), and during this period, made a documentary about the War, which was eventually shown on TV. After his military service, Panahi entered university to study filmmaking, and while there, made some documentaries. He also worked as an assistant director on some feature films. After his studies, Panahi left Tehran to make films in the outer regions of the country. On returning to Tehran, he worked with Abbas Kiarostami as his assistant director on *Through the Olive Trees* (1994). Armed with a script by his mentor, Kiarostami, Panahi made his debut as a director with *The White Balloon* (1995), and subsequently went on to make *The Mirror* (1997) and his most recent film, *The Circle* (2000).

On the surface, Panahi's films offer a variation of neorealism, Iranian-style, by capturing, in his own words, the "humanitarian aspects of things." But watching the director's latest film *The Circle* (currently doing its rounds on the international film festival circuit after winning the Golden Lion at the Venice Film Festival last year), one can't help but feel that his humanitarian cinema is a cloak, masking an even greater obsession. His motif of the circle—the camera beginning from a single point and revolving around characters only to return to the point where it began—aptly describes that obsession, expressed as much as possible through the form of the *plan séquence* (a long uninterrupted take). The circle is both a metaphor for life as well as a form that the director has subscribed to as his most representative style. Stressing the equal importance of both form and content, Panahi asserts that his work is about "humanity and its struggle," or the need for human beings to break through the confines of the circle.

In his own rather startling way, Panahi's films redefine the humanitarian themes of contemporary Iranian cinema, firstly, by treating the problems of women in modern Iran, and secondly, by depicting human characters as "non-specific persons"—more like figures who nevertheless remain full-blooded characters, holding on to the viewer's attention and gripping the senses. Like the best Iranian directors who have won acclaim on the world stage, Panahi evokes humanitarianism in an unsentimental, realistic fashion, without necessarily overriding political and social messages. In essence, this has come to define the particular aesthetic of Iranian cinema. So powerful is this sensibility that we seem to have no other mode of looking at Iranian cinema other than to equate it with a universal concept of humanitarianism.

The Circle works on the level of interpreting "humanitarian events in a poetic or artistic way," as the director himself defines his own version of neo-realist cinema. But the film is a far bolder work than most recent Iranian films; and one measure of its boldness is the fact that it is banned in Iran. It chronicles the stories of seven women, not all of whom are connected to each other, but whose fates are invariably interrelated through a circle of repression. The film works as a riveting, compelling testament about the lowly status of women in Iranian society, and about the subtle means with which Iran as a whole exercises its repression over the female sex. Panahi is, however, ambivalent about the political content of *The Circle*. In the following interview, it comes as no surprise that Panahi prefers to accentuate the human dignity of his characters—a human right that seems trivial in the context of Western society but one which is readily denied in unexpected circumstances and situations, as Panahi himself found out, to his cost. On his way to the Buenos Aires International Festival of Independent Cinema, on April 15, 2001, after having attended the Hong Kong International Film Festival, Panahi was arrested in JFK Airport, New York City, for not possessing a transit visa. Refusing to submit to a fingerprinting process (apparently required under US law), the director was handcuffed and leg-chained after much protestation to US immigration officers over his bona fides, and finally led to a plane that took him back to Hong Kong. As far as is known, this incident was not reported in any major US newspaper,[1] even though *The Circle* was being shown in the United States at the time (another irony: for that film, Panahi was awarded the "Freedom of Expression Award" by the US National Board of Review of Motion Pictures).

This interview with Jafar Panahi was conducted in Hong Kong on April 11, 2001, on the occasion of the 25th Hong Kong International Film Festival, which presented *The Circle,* among other new Iranian films. On being invited to the

Festival, the director encountered problems in securing a visa from the Chinese embassy in Tehran to enter Hong Kong (a fact that he made known to his audience whilst introducing *The Circle*). He was granted a visa only upon the intervention of the Hong Kong Festival, which made clear to the embassy that Panahi was an eminent film director and that his visit to the territory was purely a cultural one. Clearly, the case of Jafar Panahi illustrates a modern paradox: his nationality is no guarantee of decent, "humanitarian" treatment outside of Iran (the country being demonized by the international community, so to speak), even though Iranian cinema—with Panahi himself as one of its most distinguished exponents—is perhaps the most humanitarian in the world today.

Apparently, Panahi is very much focused on this paradox, taking every opportunity to decry the poor treatment (either perceived or real) that he has received when travelling out of Iran (in Hong Kong, he voiced his discontent with the Chinese embassy during interviews with the press; and similarly, the director has spoken out against his "inhuman" treatment by the US immigration authorities in JFK Airport). Through his films, Panahi expounds the humanity of all his characters, good or bad, expressing the fundamental need for decent, humanist behavior on the part of all. An indication of his focus may be gleaned from the interview itself. For instance, I began the interview by asking Panahi to define the aesthetics of Iranian cinema as he saw it. Perhaps a bit put off by the more intellectual tone of my question, Panahi went on to say that the aesthetics of Iranian cinema was married to the realistic, the actual: "the humanitarian aspects of things." Although the interview was conducted with the help of an interpreter, I could sense Panahi's stalwart personality, his total conviction about "humanity and its struggle," and his pride over what he has achieved in Iranian cinema. The case of Jafar Panahi will not be closed for a long while yet.

• • •

Stephen Teo: I would like you to begin by talking about the aesthetics of Iranian cinema. What I am struck by in all the Iranian films we have seen is the fact that they are very close to being a kind of documentary reality of Iran. But on the other hand, they're very beautiful to look at, unlike most realist-based cinemas— beautiful in the sense that they're not rough, shot with hand-held cameras with no lights, such as the neo-realist style of Italian cinema after the war. Could you give a definition of the aesthetics of Iranian cinema? How does it differ from the neo-realist style, for example?

Jafar Panahi: The Iranian cinema treats social subjects. Because you're showing social problems, you want to be more realistic and give the actual, the real aesthetics of the situation. If the audience feels the same as what they see, then they would be more sympathetic. Because you're talking about the humanitarian aspects of things, it will touch your heart. We talk about small events or small things, but it's very deep and it's very wide—things that are happening in life. According to this model, it has a poetic way and an artistic way. This may be one of the differences between Iranian movies and the movies of other countries: humanitarian events interpreted in a poetic and artistic way. In a world where films are made with millions of dollars, we made a film about a little girl who wants to buy a fish for less than a dollar (in *The White Balloon*)—this is what we're trying to show.

Whatever shows the truth of the society, in a very artistic way—that will find its own neo-realism. But this depends on the period. In Italy, neo-realism was defined by its time after the war. And now in Iran, that kind of neo-realism is disappearing.

ST: I would like to ask about your use of the idea of the circle, in *The Circle* and also in *The White Balloon*. As in *The Circle*, *The White Balloon* also uses the motif of the circle. We watch in the beginning something happen and then it's like drawing a circle, it connects with a character, an event, and then it comes back to the circle. So, what is it about this use of the circle that appeals to you?

JP: In the first *plan-séquence* in *The White Balloon,* the camera starts from those people who're playing the tambourines as they enter a shop. Somebody comes out of the shop and the camera follows him and then there's a jeep and the camera follows the jeep. The camera then arrives at a woman who goes to a balloon seller. If you have followed any one of these people, you would have arrived at the same point. It is like a wall within which they are living together, and their lives are intertwined. That little girl is like an excuse, that all these lives can be touched. But these are the lives of children. Through the eyes of children, it's a much nicer world that they see, because children are in a world where they are not really aware of the difficulties of adults. They're trying to achieve their ideals. But in the life of adults, like in *The Circle,* the characters come out of idealism and they're more realistic—they are the same children but now they have grown up and they see the world with realistic eyes.

All three films, *The White Balloon*, *The Mirror* and *The Circle*, are like full cycles—or circles—where the characters are facing up to problems, and they are trying to get out of their boundaries. In *The Circle,* we're specifically talking about, addressing, these cycles. The form also has become like a circle. We start from an opening and we go back to the same point. We start from a birth and we go through darkness. In this movie we start from one birth, the birth of a human being, and we go back again to this same point. I had the idea of this form from a racetrack, like running a 400m relay. The runners come back to the first point. If they win they win together, if they lose they lose together. But in reality it's the victory of one person.

Coming back to your first question: why is Iranian film so beautiful? When you want to say something like this and then you add an artistic form to it, you can see the circle in everything. Now our girl has become an idealistic person and thinks that she can reach for what she wants, so we open up a wide angle and we see the world through her eyes, wider, we carry the camera with the hand and we are moving just like her. When we get to the other person, the camera lens closes, the light becomes darker and it becomes slower. Then we reach the last person, there's no other movement; it's just still. If there's any movement, it's in the background. This way, the form and whatever you are saying becomes one: a circle both in the form and in the content.

ST: So the form of the circle is both a metaphor for life as well as your own style of filmmaking?
JP: Yes.

ST: When you have this circle, there's a lot of repetition. You watch the characters doing the same thing every time. And this is something that appears not only in your films but also in many other Iranian films that I've seen, for example in Kiarostami's films: he always repeats and repeats.
JP: Normally, an artist has one thing to say, and this is being expressed in different ways. But you don't see this as all being in the same shape. I'm making films about humanity and its struggle. This human being is trying to open up the circle that he encounters. Once when he is a child, and sometimes as an older person. This is what is being said in *The White Balloon,* that is, the understanding of a child. There might be ten other movies like that: they all have the same theme but you will enjoy each of them in a different way. In literature, there is also the same thing—for example, García Márquez of *100 Years of Solitude.* He's always talking about the same subject but in a different way. All artists are the same: we talk about one subject but in different ways. This is not repetition. This is the way they express it, how they see the world.

ST: I take your point, particularly when I'm watching your films. I see characters reacting, showing different emotions; so although there is repetition within the circle, I see that the characters, their emotions and gestures are different. Are you more concerned with human behavior or are you more concerned with the narrative?
JP: We must contain all. It's what we accept from this that is important. It's both of these that make an identity. Two different things: the things that are said and

the things that are acted are two different things. Sometimes they're similar. This is how you understand the personality of the person. You have to focus on both of these so that you get the character.

ST: In *The Circle*, which character do you identify with most?
JP: I like all of them in different ways, that's why I created them. The first girl is young and very idealistic. It's what comes out of her age. Or the last person who has come to the end of her life and has accepted the conditions of her life. All of them are very important. But I myself don't like to think of a person accepting his or her conditions in life. I prefer that even in a closed circle, they still try to break out of that circle. But I accept that I have to be realistic. I have to accept that in a society there are people who accept their conditions.

ST: The subject matter of *The Circle* is controversial. You mentioned that the film is still banned in Iran. In fact, when I was watching the film, I realized that through the characters, there's a lot of fear about the system, the establishment, the police. The women can't smoke; they have to wear the *chador*; they seem to want to hide every time. This is all very clear from watching the film. Did you deliberately want to make a statement about the political situation in Iran?
JP: I have to tell you again that I'm not a political person. I don't like political movies. But I take every opportunity to comment on the social issues. I talk about the current issues. To me it's not important what is the reason for what has happened. Whether it's political reasons or geographical reasons: these are not important—but the condition, the social issues. It is important to me to talk about the plight of humanity at that time. I don't want to give a political view, or start a political war. I think that the artist should rise above this. Political movies have limited time. After that time, it doesn't say anything anymore. But if the whole thing is said in an artistic way, then it doesn't have an expiration date. So it doesn't really serve a political purpose. Then it can be everlasting, for always, and it could be for anywhere. But I know that politically, with the film authorities, with any kind of film that has some political background in it, they would take issue with it. And for this reason, that is what the problem is.

ST: Still, your film makes a very strong statement about the problems that women face in Iran.
JP: Yes, I agree with that.

ST: So that is humanitarian, of course, but it's also political.
JP: Yes, I agree with that. It has the elements. It all depends on how you look at it. If a person has only political views, then he will only see the political. But if you

are a poet or an artist, then you see other things as well in the movie. If you are a socialist, you see political or economic or whatever different points of view. You mustn't look at a film with only one point of view. If you want to see *The Circle* as political, then it is one of the most political movies in Iran. By political, I mean partisan politics. But even the police, I didn't want to show them as bad. In the first instance, you are afraid of the police. Because you are looking at them from the point of view of someone who is now in prison. And normally you see him in a long shot, but when they come nearer and you see them in a medium shot, you can see their human faces. Then it comes down to, "Do you need any help?" But he goes back again and becomes frightening. If I were being political, then I would always show the police as dangerous or bad persons.

ST: In a long shot.

JP: In a long shot I would show them rough. A political person can only see black or white. But I intertwine the tones. This is where the humanitarian eye comes in. I don't want to bring somebody down or say, "Death to this, or life to that."

ST: I've seen *The White Balloon* and *The Circle*: they're both films about women. Obviously you feel a lot about the problems of women.

JP: I don't really know—but probably it was due to the fact that my first film was made with a very low budget, and I thought it would be easier to work with children. I thought that filming with children would meet with fewer problems with the censors. Perhaps too, at that time, I had my own children, and it went automatically down that road. I have both a boy and a girl and I can see that the girl can strike up relationships in an easier, milder way. So I thought that a girl could give a better impression. Then when I finished the film and I started *The Mirror*, I began to think about what happens now that the girl has grown up in society. And then automatically, it became a movie about women. It started unconsciously but now the question is settled.

ST: So now you have made a trilogy about women. They are all linked.

JP: I agree.

ST: Shall we talk a bit about the process of making your film? You use both amateurs and professionals?

JP: I haven't really tried to be either this way or that way. I just choose. I just try to see what roles I have and who they would fit. I look for the person who fits what is in my mind. I know that to bring the professional and amateur together is very difficult. The acting must be on the same level. At this point, normally it is more difficult for the professional, because the professional has to come down and adapt to the level of the amateurs. The amateur is not role playing but doing what comes naturally. So the professional has not to give a performance, but to learn how to be more natural.

ST: So how long did it take to make your film?
JP: Fifty-three days from beginning to end. In the middle, there were about eighteen days when we didn't work, usually because the weather wasn't good. There were thirty-seven days of filming.

ST: Were there a lot of rehearsals?
JP: The first *plan-séquence* was repeated thirteen times, the shot from the hospital to the street. The cameraman would film the scene and take the shot back to the laboratory to check it and then he would re-shoot it again. This was repeated thirteen times until we got what we wanted. This is one of the difficulties of doing long sequences like this. If I had wanted to break it down, I could have done it in half a day. That sequence took about five days. There were seven to eight such long takes in the film.

ST: Who conceived the script?
JP: Myself. Took about a year. Then, I wrote the different characters—where they come from and where they go to, which took about two months.

ST: Was it based on a story or a novel?
JP: Original script.

ST: And all your films are original scripts?
JP: Yes.

ST: That's very remarkable. What about the photography? Do you handle the camera?
JP: I have a camera operator. But I do the editing.

ST: There are many elements in the film that remind me of folk culture. Like the end scene, where the prostitute is in the prison van and there's a fellow prisoner, a man who starts to sing, reminiscent of folk music or folk culture. And also in *The White Balloon* where the girl comes out in the street and there's the snake charmer. Do you consciously want to show all these elements?
JP: When you see the film with subtitles, you don't understand the original language. If you could understand, you would know that everyone has a different

accent, like a folk song or folk dance from a different part of Iran. These accents and these tones of folk culture also help to make the film more attractive. Tehran is a very big city and there are people from all over Iran living in the city. This is one of the features of a big city. The people in the film help one another so that they are believable and true, and sometimes I do this purposely—like the three girls who were playing their guitars—they're speaking in the Azerbaijani language, and the young girl who is one of the three women in the beginning, also has an Azerbaijani accent. And when she's sitting in front of the painting, and talking about the countryside that she sees in the painting, she's actually talking about Azerbaijan. So there are all kinds of connections. That painting was something from Van Gogh, for example. I chose it because it was not a specific geographic place. It could be anywhere in the world, but it was inspired by an actual painting by Van Gogh. I wanted to say that where you want to be could be anywhere in the world.

ST: I want to ask about the three female characters in the beginning. I'm not sure what exactly they went to prison for.

JP: It doesn't matter. It could be anything you want. That's not important. It's a very delicate point. If I had decided to give them some crime that they were guilty of, like something political or because of drugs, they would become specific persons. But they are not specific persons. You can have anybody there. Then the problem is a much larger problem. Maybe if it were a specific person there would be no censorship. But when it's open to interpretation, then it's more difficult. If it was a specific person, the censors can then say this person has this kind of crime, then it's not a problem. Because I wanted the audience to think for themselves, I left it open to interpretation.

ST: What is your next project?

JP: This was such a difficult film for me. We wanted very much to show this film. In the past six months from the start of the first showing, I've always been travelling. I've been to many different countries in Asia, Europe, North America, Africa— long trips. I haven't had time to think about the next project.

ST: Having travelled all over the world now, do you think that being a filmmaker in Iran is much more difficult than in other countries?

JP: Every country has its own difficulties. In some countries, it's a budget problem. In other countries, it's political problems. And in some places, it's a lack of knowledge about the movie industry. In some places, there are tools but there are no people. In other places, there are people but no tools to make films with. There are problems everywhere, in different shapes.

ST: Just to focus on Iran. For example, what are the censorship problems that you face?

JP: There's censorship in Iran and China—both closed countries and closed societies.

ST: Is it much more difficult to want to make a film about women in Iran?

JP: It is a problem, but there are about sixty movies made every year in Iran, and ten or fifteen of them are about women. We have women directors, making movies about women. In a society governed by men, these problems do exist.

ST: Do you practice self-censorship?

JP: Never. Whatever I want to say, I try to say it. If I were my own censor, then I may not have any problems. At first they didn't allow me to make the movie. We took about ten months. In the end, they gave me permission to make the movie. They gave me a letter and in the letter they said that after the film was made, they would evaluate it to see whether it could be shown. I forgot about the letter. I thought that I would make the movie first and then decide what to do about the situation. If I had paid attention to the letter, I would have to be my own censor and maybe then, I would have been able to show my film in Iran.

ST: Would you call your film a documentary or a drama?

JP: It's a drama that has become a documentary.

ST: Have you heard of the term "docu-drama"?

JP: I make my film, then you name it.

• • •

The input and assistance of Mr. Shahrukh Borumand in the preparation of this article is gratefully acknowledged.

Notes

1. For example, Jonathan Rosenbaum in his review of *The Circle* states that no major US newspaper made mention of this incident or reprinted Panahi's statement to the US National Board of Review of Motion Pictures.

An Open Letter to the US National Board of Review of Motion Pictures

Jafar Panahi / 2001

Dear Ladies and Gentlemen,

As the winner of the Freedom of Expression Award for my film *The Circle,* I would like to draw your kind attention to what happened to me in your country, an incident that takes place every day in the US, and let me hope to see your reaction to these inhumane incidents. I believe I am entitled to be curious about the response of the Board that granted me such an Award, a response I hope will be in proportion to the treatment I and many other people faced and will no doubt continue to face.

You have hailed my film as "wonderful and daring"; I wish your Board and the US media would dare to condemn the savage acts of American police/Immigration officers and that such condemnation would make people aware of these practices. Otherwise, what would winning such an award mean for me? And what honor would I have in keeping it?

In the booklet you kindly sent me with your award, I read that prestigious film personality Orson Welles had also previously received this award. Should I be happy that this great man is not among us now to hear how the American police behave toward filmmakers or people who enter your country? As a filmmaker obsessed with social issues, my films deal with social problems and limitations, and naturally I cannot be indifferent to racist, violent, insulting, and inhumane treatment in any place in the world. However, I am careful to separate the actions of US Customs from the cultural institutions and great people of the US—indeed, I was informed that my film was very well-received by film critics and audiences in your country. Nevertheless, I will inform the world media about my unpleasant experience in New York, and I hope your Board, which stands for freedom of expression, will react properly in this respect.

•••

On April 15, I left the Hong Kong Film Festival to go to the Montevideo and Bue-nos Aires Festivals on United Airlines' flight 820. This thirty-hour trip was via New York's JFK airport, where I had a two-hour layover before my next flight to Montevideo. Per my request, the staff of both festivals had already confirmed that a transit visa was not required for this route, and moreover the airline issued me the ticket visa for New York. When I asked the United Airlines staff if I needed to have a transit visa for the Hong Kong airport, I heard the same response.

As soon as I arrived at JFK airport, American customs police took me to an office and asked to fingerprint and photograph me because of my nationality. I refused to do it and I showed them my invitations to the festivals. They threatened to put me in jail if I would not do the fingerprinting. I asked for an interpreter and to make a phone call. They refused. Then, they chained me like a prisoner from medieval times and put me in a police patrol, taking me to another part of the airport. There were many people, women and men from different countries. They passed me to new policemen, who chained my feet and locked my chain to the others, all of us locked to a very dirty bench. For ten hours, we were not per-mitted to ask questions and were given no answers, forced to sit on that bench, pressed to each other. I could not move and I was suffering from an old ailment, but nobody would take notice. Again, I requested that they let me call someone in New York, but they refused. They not only ignored my request but also that of a boy from Sri Lanka who wanted to call his mom. Everybody was moved by the crying of the boy—people from Mexico, Peru, Eastern Europe, India, Pakistan, Bangladesh—and I was thinking that any country has its own laws, but I just could not understand this barbaric treatment.

At last, I saw the next morning. Another policeman came to me and said that they have to take my photograph. I said never and showed them my personal photos. They said no, they have to take my photo (in the way criminals are photo-graphed) and do the fingerprinting. I refused. An hour later, two other guys came to me and threatened to do the fingerprinting and photography by computer, and again I refused, this time asking for a phone. At last, they accepted and I called Dr. Jamsheed Akrami, the Iranian film professor at Columbia University. I explained the whole story and asked him to convince customs—and he knows me well—that I am not a criminal or someone they're looking for.

Two hours later, a policeman came to me and took my personal photos. They chained me again and took me to a plane, a plane that was going back to Hong Kong. In the plane and from my window, I could see New York. I knew my film *The Circle* had been released there for two days and had been very well received, too. However, the audiences would understand my film better if they could know that its director was at that moment chained in their own country. They would appre-ciate my belief that the circles that limit human freedoms do exist in all parts of this world but with different ratios. I saw the Statue of Liberty outside the window and I unconsciously smiled. I tried to draw the curtain and there were scars of the chain on my hand. I could not stand the other travelers gazing at me and I just wanted to stand up and cry, "I'm not a thief! I'm not a murderer! I'm not a drug dealer! I . . . I am just an Iranian, a filmmaker." But how could I convey this and in what language? In Chinese, Japanese, or the mother tongues of those people from Mexico, Peru, Russia, India, Pakistan, Bangladesh . . . or in the language of that young boy from Sri Lanka? Really, in what language?

I had not slept for sixteen hours and I had to spend another fifteen hours on my way back to Hong Kong. It was pure torture among all those watching eyes. I closed my eyes and tried to sleep. But I could not. I could only see the images of those sleepless women and men who were still chained.

Crime and Self-Punishment in Tehran

Richard Porton / 2003

From *Cinema Scope* No. 17 (January 12, 2003): 9–13. Reprinted by permission of Andrew Tracy, Managing Editor, *Cinema Scope*.

Though it may be a hoary cliché, "deceptive simplicity" is an uncannily accurate phrase to describe Jafar Panahi's *Crimson Gold*. Like many films by Panahi's mentor and occasional screenwriter Abbas Kiarostami, *Crimson Gold* might be misinterpreted as a straightforward piece of social realism. Playfully torn, with numerous modifications, from yesterday's headlines, the film recounts a poor pizza delivery-man's botched robbery of a jewelry store and his subsequent suicide. Instead of leading up to this heist gone awry in a linear fashion, Panahi short circuits any possibility of suspense by bracketing the narrative with this decisive event. The bulk of the film, however, is preoccupied with more mundane slices of daily Iranian life, such as ill-fated protagonist Hussein's (Hossain Emadeddin) purse-snatching excursions and a quasi-surreal tête-à-tête between Hussein and a rich customer who shows little interest in his pizza order and spouts misogynistic invective with casual glee. Hussein is a quintessentially marginal antihero. A bearish, sullen man whose halting speech makes him appear strangely pensive, he may strike audiences accustomed to romantic portrayals of outcasts as a de facto political rebel. In the end, he is not a rebel, villain, or hero, but an unsentimentalized victim who seals his own doom.

While Panahi oddly claims that he is a "social," not a "political," filmmaker, there is a clear rationale for this assertion. While a Western director who would say such a thing risks being branded an apolitical humanist, Panahi simultaneously acknowledges the political implications of his work while refusing to be pigeonholed as anything so constricting as a mere realist, modernist, or dissident filmmaker. Of course, as was true of Eastern European directors during the era of state socialism, the simple decision to make a film that can be construed as critical of the Iranian regime is automatically a political act. (*Crimson Gold* has been banned in Iran and, like many nonconformist Iranians, Panahi is frequently interrogated by the authorities.)

But, as Gilberto Perez observes in a *London Review of Books* essay on Hamid Dabashi's *Close Up: Iranian Cinema Past, Present, and Future,* in the West, "By and large aesthetics has become divorced from ethics, art from the things that matter in real life—Iranian cinema knows no such split." For this reason, as Perez emphasizes in his writing on Kiarostami, it is absurd to separate Iranian cinema's neorealist tendencies from its modernist predilections. From this vantage point, *Crimson Gold* is a social-realist film that refuses to partake of the pat didacticism that often mars the pedestrian, if well-intentioned "social problem" films of, say, Martin Ritt and Costa-Gavras. Panahi's brand of social commentary is more meditative than sermonizing, and shares more with cinematic modernism than neorealism.

As Panahi makes abundantly clear, *Crimson Gold* is not reducible to a monolithic cluster of themes or motifs. The bravura opening sequence—which features a static long take of the robbery and suicide from Hussein's point of view—is a departure point (which Panahi will return to, in a characteristically circular fashion, at the end of the film) that allows him to explore the hidden crevices of Iranian society. His previous film, *The Circle* (2000), drove home its dissection of the oppression of Iranian women by rhyming opening and closing shots—sliding door panels of a hospital and a prison. For *The Circle*'s ostracized female protagonists—unwed mothers and prostitutes eluding the authorities in Tehran—the long arm of the state extends beyond prison bars. Just as it is impossible to extract a simplistic message from Panahi's cinematic modus operandi, it is equally difficult to glibly analyze Hussein's mental anguish or his personal motivations; the film is as anti-psychological as it is undidactic. Panahi speaks frequently of "playing" with viewers and allowing them to make up their own minds (what could be more modernist?) and the film might be best enjoyed as a series of provocations that hint at social or psychological insights without spelling them out in a tediously literal-minded fashion. The humiliation that Hussein experiences when a jewelry-store owner treats him with haughty condescension, the shadowy figures at a forbidden party witnessed from the street by Hussein and a weary soldier, and the hearty belch that reverberates on the film's soundtrack as the forlorn deliveryman digests pizza in the home of a wealthy customer, all coalesce to provide a succinct view of a society where an underground economy thrives, the regime's mores are spurned in private on a daily basis, yet a rigid class structure remains intact. But connecting the dots between these incidents requires multiple viewings.

Since Panahi cancelled his trip to the New York Film Festival as a protest against the US government's harassment of Iranian citizens, his visit to the Toronto International Film Festival became the only opportunity for Panahi to discuss his work's artistic and political implications. He gave the impression of a man wedged between two authoritarian regimes—an Iran that treats him as a dangerous subversive and a United States that views him as a potential terrorist. As he wrote in a letter to

New York Film Festival director Richard Peña explaining his decision to protest the Immigration and Naturalization Service's policy of finger-printing Iranian nationals: "We live in strange times. It's not just George Bush who subscribes to the idea that you are either with us or against us. In my country, too, anyone slightly crossing red lines is subject to the suspicion of the censors who label him as being alienated, self-loathing, mercenary, infiltrator, enemy agent, and even heretic. In Iran they interrogate me because I am a socially conscious filmmaker. In America, they fingerprint me, and literally shackle me to kill my national pride, because I am an Iranian filmmaker."

Richard Porton: According to what I've read, *Crimson Gold* is partially based on an actual incident. Could you comment on the differences and similarities between that incident and the film's narrative?

Jafar Panahi: The only true aspect of the story in the film involves the opening scene with the burglar going into the store. It's fiction playing with truth, although I try to capture the social reality of Tehran.

RP: I assume you added certain details such as making Hussein, the burglar, a pizza deliveryman. It doesn't seem likely that this character would find himself in upper-class neighborhoods if he didn't have this sort of job.

JP: I wasn't even sure of the actual robber's profession. That was only a narrative excuse to allow the character to travel within different levels of Iranian society. We always try to find an excuse in our movies to discover what's going on in various strata of society. Hussein, the main character, is just a string pulling us from the southern part of the city to northern neighborhoods. He's the catalyst.

RP: Since Abbas Kiarostami wrote the screenplay, how much of the film's conception derives from his ideas and how much is attributable to you? Or was it a thoroughgoing collaboration?

JP: I was sitting in a car with Mr. Kiarostami one day on our way to his photography exhibition. He asked, "Have you heard the story of this guy robbing the store and then committing suicide?" I left the exhibition after an hour, did some thinking and then called him. I told him that I thought this story could be the basis of a good movie—especially if we opened the film with the scene of the robbery. We travelled about five or six times to the north of Iran and had many discussions about the movie. After that point, he wrote the script. Of course, it's only natural that some aspects of the story were changed during the filming.

RP: The structure of the film seems crucial. The power of the film derives from the decision to have the robbery bookend the film, and you just mentioned that this was your idea. The importance of point of view also seems unavoidable—the fact that, for much of the film, we're seeing events through Hussein's eyes.

JP: Yes, that's right. That's why we're with Hussein throughout the film. If he doesn't see something, the audience won't see it either. We never go anywhere without Hussein.

RP: And you always wanted to open the film with a static shot of the robbery from Hussein's point of view.

JP: That's correct; I always emphasize one person's point of view in all of my films. In *The Circle,* for example, once we leave one person and his or her point of view we go on to the next character and leave the previous perspective behind.

RP: All of your films seem to take a very simple concept as the departure point. These broad concepts leave you a lot of room for exploration within an initial schema.

JP: Exactly. For example, in *The White Balloon* (1996) and *The Mirror* (1997)—two films about children—the camera rarely travels further than their eye line and point of view. Their world is of course much smaller than the adults' world. When the eye line goes higher to capture the world of the adults, the children disappear. Then the ugly face of truth reveals itself; things get harsher when an innocent perspective vanishes from the scene.

RP: I've read that you were greatly impressed by Hitchcock's films. And of course he's a master at controlling a tightly focused point of view.

JP: Yes, when I was at the university I watched all of his movies. When I first became interested in making movies, I slavishly imitated Hitchcock's editing style. When I made movies in his style, I noticed that they seemed perfect technically but were soulless and lacked humanity. Maybe I felt that the films were detached from reality. I then tried to move from attempting technical perfection and attempted to capture reality. At that point, the camera's no longer as important. When you have the right story and concept, technical prowess is no longer important. After I discovered Hitchcock, I was also inspired by many other directors— Buñuel, Godard, and the neorealists.

RP: You could say that there's always a tension between a classical style and what could be called a "neorealist" tendency in your films.

JP: That all comes down to the viewer's perceptions. I just make the films. All directors are influenced by previous directors and hope to make an impact on directors who will make films in the future. Being influenced by other directors doesn't mean copying their style; you're inspired to create your own style.

RP: Unlike in your other films, we don't see many women in *Crimson Gold*. Nevertheless, we hear many conversations about women. Is this a strategy of indirection as well? And what is the source of the rich man's extreme misogyny?

JP: Yes. I think you're right about my strategy. Of course, this rich man (Pourang) might refer to the woman who has visited him as a prostitute, but she's obviously not one since he also mentioned the possibility of marriage. Because Pourang has lived for such a long time in the United States, he doesn't understand that women in Iran are expected to get married before becoming acquainted with men. According to the religious precepts, you're required to be married before becoming intimate.

RP: Your films always focus on urban life in Tehran. Was it particularly important for you to use this setting to focus on class distinctions in *Crimson Gold*?

JP: It's not only about social levels—that's only one, perhaps limited, perspective on the film. Easterners are more concerned with being insulted than with the differences between rich and poor. Hussein doesn't really have a problem with the upper class. If he wanted to, he could have robbed the house of the rich guy he visits. But, when he goes to the fancy jewelry store and the owner doesn't let him in, he feels insulted. I never wanted to be preoccupied with class distinctions within Iranian society. I merely wanted to show that each class has its own problems.

RP: In other words, his humiliation at the hands of the shop owner is the primary catalyst that eventually makes him snap.

JP: That could be one of the main causes for his breakdown. It might also be related to his social life. And there might be other causes as well. It's just the nature of Iranian cinema to leave the matter open and allow the viewer to think. Viewers can construct their own version of the story in their heads. They can translate whatever happens to the character into a narrative that fits their own lives and is comprehensible to them. Maybe that's the main difference between Hollywood movies and Iranian movies.

RP: This open-ended narrative tendency seems particularly striking towards the end of the film. There's an elliptical transition between Hussein's sojourn in the rich man's house back to the robbery without any obvious causal link. The viewer has to determine what's ensued between these two sequences.

JP: Yes, there is really no need to explain the transition because when Hussein jumps in the water at the rich man's apartment he feels pure. Then he makes the decision to commit the robbery. It doesn't really matter how he gets from one place to another.

RP: How, in precise terms, does he feel pure?

JP: He feels cleansed. Water is a symbol of purity. He can become a new man when cleansed and he can make new decisions. This is true from both a religious and a geographical, nonreligious perspective. He doesn't even touch anything after this point; he sits and waits for the sun to come up. I actually shot a scene—included in the original script—which depicts him following the jeweler after he drops off his grandson at school. But then I took it out since it didn't seem necessary to me.

RP: You've always featured nonprofessionals in your films. I understand, for example, that the man who plays Hussein is a schizophrenic.

JP: That's true; he has a mental problem. Most of my actors have been nonprofessionals. And the actor who plays Hussein actually is a pizza deliveryman. He wouldn't agree to act in the movie initially and kept us waiting for a few months. Then we went through his brother, a doctor, who eventually convinced him to act in the movie.

RP: Was it difficult to work with such a troubled man?

JP: It was very, very difficult. Because of his illness, he had certain problems and it was occasionally impossible to continue filming. At certain times, it became unbearable. There were two or three occasions when I was almost ready to abandon this movie. But I eventually regained hope and was able to carry on. When I realized that it was occasionally difficult to include him in certain scenes because of his illness, I decided that if we concentrated totally on his point of view the audience wouldn't actually need to see him at certain times. Filming in sequence also helped me to maintain his point of view throughout the movie.

RP: Do you usually shoot in sequence?

JP: Since the actors are often nonprofessionals, I usually shoot in sequence. They can't stay in character and find their place within the story if the movie isn't shot in sequence. The only times I can't shoot in sequence are when I'm on location or re-shooting certain scenes.

RP: I suppose your shooting style might be different if you worked primarily with professional actors.

JP: That's true; most of the time we don't even give the actors a screenplay. So they usually don't know what they'll have to do the next day. They follow the story as the audience does. I believe that Hussein (Emadeddin) was the only nonprofessional actor who was given the screenplay. Considering his illness, I feared that he was going to come up with an excuse to leave the movie. I thought I could placate him with the script. When he read the script, however, he told me that he didn't like it!

RP: Did he stick to the lines you'd given him, or did he improvise?
JP: Sometimes he stuck to the lines and sometimes he forgot them. We tried to incorporate his behavior into the character.

RP: How do you explain the significance of the film's slightly opaque title?
JP: It's one of those titles that involves playing with the audience. For example, in *The White Balloon* you never actually glimpse a white balloon. We hope the title triggers certain associations in the audience. Sometimes the titles are metaphorical and sometimes not. It's similar to the way the film is constructed—with the rhyming of the ending and the beginning. Gold is a symbol of wealth and crimson is a symbol of blood. So we're saying to the audience in advance that they can expect both wealth and blood.

RP: Can you talk about some other games being played with the audience? In the rich man's house, some red spots we assume are blood turn out to be nail polish.
JP: Yes. That's right.

RP: You seem to delight in suggesting what goes on behind closed doors. As in the scene featuring Hussein and the rich man, we view, albeit in shadow, a party—which is technically illegal—as Hussein and a soldier converse outside. In other words, the schism between the private and public realms certainly plays an important role in the film.
JP: That's one of the problems in our real lives. When young people want to hold a party, they're putting themselves in great danger. So Hussein acts as a narrative device that allows us to display problems of this kind. The party is also there as something unreachable for those two guys. They can stand outside and realize there's a party going on, but they'll never access that world.

RP: Because of their position in society?
JP: It's partly that and also the fact that, as a filmmaker in Iran, I'm not allowed to go inside and shoot that sort of party. So it's shot obliquely. Even having a party in Iran is considered a crime.

RP: Of course, I understand that parties of this kind are quite common in Iran.
JP: That's true, there are always parties. But it's also true that, only two weeks ago, the police followed a young man and woman who were leaving a party. They shot at the couple and the boy was killed.

RP: Ironically enough, although you're not able to shoot an actual party, this limitation could be considered an aesthetic advantage. In the end, it's more dramatically effective.

JP: That's true. Even if I was able to make a movie that featured a couple making love, I might choose not to. I think it's more effective, for me at least, to shoot outside closed doors.

An Interview with Jafar Panahi, Director of *Crimson Gold*

David Walsh / 2003

From *World Socialist Web Site* (wswb.org), September 17, 2003. Reprinted by permission.

David Walsh: This is an Iranian film with an obvious international significance. In the US such tragedies happen every day. Unfortunately, one almost becomes accustomed to them. What was it about this particular incident that caught your attention?

Jafar Panahi: It's true that when you live in a society like ours, things like that happen all the time, but there are certain times, certain moments, certain days, when you hear what happens, the pain hits you so hard, you think about it seriously. It's like when you take the same route from home to work every day and one day you notice for the first time something that was always there. You focus on it. It causes you pain and you think you have to do something about it.

So as a filmmaker, when I heard what happened it struck me and I had to do something about it. We were going to Kiarostami's photographic exhibition. When he told me what happened, I could not stay at the exhibition any longer and I felt I had to do something. I can't even remember what kind of emotional feeling I had that day.

The party scene in the movie, when the police raid, happens all the time, and young people are always struggling with the problem and they get arrested, and their parents sign papers that they won't do it again. Three weeks ago, something happened in Tehran. Although it was a very sad thing, I felt pleased that I had exposed this in my movie. Three weeks ago, after a party, the police followed a boy and girl, and fired at them, and the boy was killed. As a social filmmaker, I respond to whatever is happening in our social life.

Although the people living in that society are totally used to what happened at the party, it is necessary to expose it and show it again as a real problem.

Because the Iranian government is based on religion, any relationship between boys and girls—if they're not married, if they're dancing together at a party—is a crime. So they have to do something about it. Sometimes they have the proper papers and they have permission to raid the house. And sometimes they wait outside for people to come out—they can also catch more people like that.

DW: Is the question of social inequality a subject that is discussed by filmmakers, journalists and politicians in Iran? It is a major fact of life in the US, but hardly anyone talks about it or makes films about it.

JP: Inequality exists in every country of the world. But a certain point can be reached ... there is no middle class anymore, because of wrong political decisions or economic problems. And then the gap between poor and rich gets bigger, and that's how it is right now. That causes violence and aggravation. And the various people who are struggling with this problem react differently. Hussein was not a thief; if he had been, he would have stolen from the rich man. He wanted to defend his humanity against humiliation. We don't want to say whether it's right or wrong. But we say that's how it is.

DW: The film showed me many things about Iran for the first time. We have never seen such wealthy homes before. Was that deliberate, to show such wealth?

JP: Yes, and that's the way it is because of the gap that's getting bigger between rich and poor. And the characters in the movie don't even compare to the really wealthy people in Iran.

DW: There is not simply the economic effect, but the psychological and emotional impact, and not only on the poor. Did you also want to speak about the consequences for those with money?

JP: I want to show people at every level of society, and I want to show their problems. I don't want to say that people at one level of society are better or worse off. We have about four to five million Iranian people who live outside Iran; they left the country after the revolution. Most of them were children when they fled the country, and they don't have any real knowledge about what's happening in Iran now. But as they love their country, they always want to go back and try to live there. But when they come back, they can't relate to people and they suffer. That's why he invited Hussein in, so they could talk about the problems. And we feel as bad for the rich guy as we do for Hussein.

DW: Hussein seems terribly injured, both by war and the economic situation. Do you feel that many Iranians have been wounded in this fashion?

JP: There is a saying that we think insane people are more fortunate, because they don't really see what's happening around them. But if you really see what's going on around you, it's going to make you suffer deeply. And that's Hussein's situation; he hardly talks, but he sees much, and when he sees something, he really sees deeply into it. And he is ill, and he suffers both physically and emotionally.

DW: Yesterday at the public screening you described yourself as an independent filmmaker. That is often a misused term in North America. What do you mean by "independent"?

JP: Independent from any kind of dependency and coercion anywhere in the world. Independent from any belief I think is not right. Refusing self-censorship and believing any movie that I make is, in the end, exactly what I wanted to say. A lot of times, when you say you're independent, it means economically, that you don't get paid by other people. But where we are, independent means more like independence from politics. That's why I don't make political movies. Because if I were a political filmmaker, then I would have to work for political parties and I would have to go along with their beliefs of what's wrong and what's right. But what I say is that art transcends politics. It rises above it. You never say what's wrong or right. We just show the problems. And it's up to the audience to decide what's wrong or right. A political movie becomes dated, but an independent artistic film never gets old and is always fresh. Although I'm making my movies in Iran as a geographical area, my voice is an international one. That's what I mean by "independent." Whenever I feel pain, I'm going to respond, because I'm not dependent on any party, and I don't take orders, and I decide independently when I make my movies. I try to struggle with all the difficulties and make my movie. If I weren't independent, I would say yes to anyone. But when I want to make a movie, I'll do anything it takes. And that's not what government officials like. And the pleasure is much greater.

DW: I congratulate you on your criticism of the situation in Iran and your refusal to come to New York because of US government policy. What is your attitude toward the invasion of Iraq?

JP: People in the Middle East aren't really optimistic about America. And all the ordinary people think that everything America does is to suit itself. And to serve its own self-interest, the US government disregards international opinion and law. We were in a war with Saddam for eight years, and America was supporting him the whole time. Saddam bombarded us with chemical weapons. But suddenly, when America saw its own interests threatened by Saddam, then they attack. We saw this in Afghanistan. When they wanted to invade Afghanistan, we had to laugh because we knew they would never find bin Laden. There is always going to be a scapegoat that Americans can use.

A Soccer Match to Imagine:
An Interview with Jafar Panahi on *Offside*

Majid Eslami / 2006

From *Haft Magazine* (Tehran) 4.29 (2006): 6–12. Translated by Hossein Eidizadeh.

Majid Eslami: To what extent is soccer part of your life?

Jafar Panahi: We have to go way back. We used to live in the south of Tehran, southwest Tehran, in the Emamzadeh Hasan neighborhood. There were plenty of empty lots there, and the cheapest hobby was playing soccer. There were many empty lots, but people didn't have enough money to invest in building. All the houses were forty to sixty square meters and people lived together like ants. Crowded houses of workers. If you wanted to stretch your legs you had to put them on somebody's head! We had to get out of the house. I had a number of hobbies, one of which was the Kanoon library, though it was far from our house. I was eleven or twelve when I wrote a short story and won a first prize there. They suggested that I join Super 8 filmmaking groups. Then I realized they were looking for a chubby boy for one of the films. I was really fat then. *The Elephant and the Teacup* was the name of the film, and I acted in it. It was one of the ways to get out. The second one was playing soccer in the area, and I was a goalkeeper on one of the teams. Moreover, we had to earn our own living. In the summer, I used to go with my father to work—he was a construction painter. I had another job as well: I used to make soft drinks in big pots and sell them in soccer stadiums. It was so cheap. My first memories of soccer date back to those days.

ME: For how long did you go to stadiums?

JP: It didn't last long. Other things were more interesting to me. I was dying to have a camera and finally I bought a Zenith camera and started taking photos. Gradually I got more interested in cinema. Cinema substituted for soccer.

ME: How long did it take you to decide to make a movie about issues surrounding soccer, which is in part about soccer and in part dealing with social issues?

JP: I wasn't thinking about making a film about soccer at all. The idea first came to me eight years ago. Together with my family, I went to welcome Iran's national team when it returned from its match against Australia. We went to Azadi stadium. At that time we lived in Shahran. When we arrived we saw so many women who were there to welcome the team and they were not allowed to enter the stadium. Something was taking shape at exactly that moment in the back of my mind. A few years later, discussions about letting women enter soccer stadiums started. I remember when Ataullah Behmanesh[1] pointed to the history of the law, saying it dated back to ancient Greece when women could have been executed for entering certain arenas. Until 400 B.C., women disguised themselves as men to enter such places and watch their sons and brothers play. And after that, this wall fell down. This was another thing, by the way, that triggered something in my mind: What would happen if women were to go to a stadium in men's clothes? The other thing was when I went with my daughter, Solmaz, who was twelve or thirteen, to watch Iran's national soccer team train. They didn't let her in. However, she somehow managed to get in. The final blow was when, in the match between Iran and Qatar, in overtime, Vahid Hashemian scored and it was clear that Iran had a great chance to go to the World Cup; at that point I got serious about making the film, as the very first ideas were shaping in my mind, and I started going to stadiums regularly and sometimes shot footage.

ME: Did you ever see a girl in boy's clothes in the stadium?

JP: No, never. However, people's reaction and the uncontrollable atmosphere in the stadium made me decide not to show the inside of the stadium. Besides, the history of cinema indicates that movies focused on what happens in stadiums are doomed.

ME: What do you think is the reason?

JP: Watching the match on television is always more interesting. Cameras record moments that you cannot see in the stadium. There are fewer dead moments, and replays of important moments help you to see a moment from different angles.

ME: I think there is another reason as well. The televised picture that we are used to is based on long shots. Details are included in them. When filmmakers like John Huston want to show us a soccer match, they deal with it through conventional means, and that is why we don't realize where the player is on the field and we may be confused.

JP: There are practical reasons as well. As a filmmaker you never have that much of an audience in the stadium, so you can do as many long shots as you want. But you can't control what happens and can't predict where the ball is going. That's why you use close-ups.

ME: And everything seems fabricated, like when Pelé scored in *Victory*.[2] If you see a score like that in a live match, it is totally exciting.
JP: Because you are living that moment. If you remember, there was a time when they broadcast soccer matches with a one-hour delay and it was not exciting. Now that they broadcast it with a few seconds delay, it is more exciting.[3] The first film I made starts with a soccer match. It was called *Pol*.[4] While making it, I realized I could not control soccer. I was trying hard to show I was in control. When the editing was finished, my editor told me it was really good. However, I felt I didn't want that film to be in my career. I stole the rushes so that no one could see it.

ME: This is the problem with sports. If you want to make a film about volleyball you will have the same problem.
JP: The problem is that you cannot control the ball. It is like an animal, and working with animals is also difficult.

ME: So you realized you wanted to make a movie about what is going on around soccer, but you couldn't focus on it.
JP: Exactly, that experience was doomed. I thought it would be great to see soccer from another point of view. I mean, listening to it and imagining it. When I saw that soldier from Mashhad standing on that wall and reporting the match for the girls, I realized it would be my fifth film.

ME: When did Shadmehr Rastin[5] join the film?
JP: I had a thirty- to forty-page treatment, and to complete it I started talking to friends who I knew were interested in soccer. I talked to film critics, cineastes. I knew Shadmehr was interested in soccer, and it had been a few years that we had been wanting to work together. I especially wanted to work with him because the film was about soccer, and when he joined us he had very good ideas.

ME: Like what?
JP: Like, when the girl escapes from the Mashhadi soldier, she was supposed to go inside the stadium and see the final minutes of the match—and in the last scene we would see the girl alone in the stadium knowing she managed to see the match. In one of my discussions with Shadmehr, we decided to take the last minutes of the game outside the stadium and see what happens there. Most of the ideas regarding scenes outside the stadium are Shadmehr's ideas. Or the idea of the soldier using the girl's cell phone. However, I don't recall who suggested many of the other ideas.

ME: How many of the scenes were shot before the Iran-Bahrain match?
JP: I remember we had a scene in a teahouse, where we see soccer fan leaders talking about what to do during the match. We didn't use that scene in the final cut. We also shot parts of the bus scene before the match.

ME: How about the match scenes?
JP: The first scenes of the girl entering the stadium were shot that day, and also the scene of people celebrating.

ME: What about the scene where the soldier goes to the rest room?
JP: Yes, it was also shot that day. We thought that in order to sympathize with the girls, we shouldn't go inside the stadium and show the match. If they have not seen it, we shouldn't see it either. Moreover, it was possible that the audience would think it was fabricated. In order to convey the sense of reality, we have two shots. One is the one you mentioned and the other is the scene where we see the old man and in the background we can see the soccer field and the fans. In this way the audience would not be suspicious. It was at Fajr Film Festival that a lot of people asked me if I shot the film in one day. And I told them, is it possible to shoot a film in one day?

ME: Would everything have changed if Bahrain had won the match?
JP: [laughter] I don't know what would have happened. My plan was, in a way, to shoot the Vanak[6] celebration scene after the stadium shoot. After shooting the entering scenes, we went with Mahmoud Kalari[7] to the section where fans sit. We wanted Iran to score in the second half of the match. But after watching the match for a few minutes, I was worried that if Iran didn't score in the first fifteen minutes, it would be really hard for the team. It was this magical moment when I told myself that the movie was not important at all, the only thing that mattered was Iran's victory! During the second half, when we were shooting, Iran scored and we were relieved. We immediately left the stadium and started shooting the celebration scenes.

ME: Were you worried when you decided to use people's own dialects in the film?
JP: I was not worried about the Azeri soldier at all. If we had used the first shots we got of him, yes, there might have been a little problem. It was important for me that the soldiers not be from Tehran. Because in a way, they are prisoners as well and they are forced to be there because of the match, exactly like the girls. I tried to walk this thin line of correctly using dialects and not mocking them.

ME: I think your film is successful in this regard, though there are comic scenes too. When the film is finished we feel the soldier is his own character. For example, in the scene where he holds the antenna, so the girls can watch the match, we see his humane side.

JP: Or when he buys drinks for everyone, and also the scene where he defends the girl in front of the old man. We didn't have that scene in the script. I added that scene to emphasize his humane character. Another thing is that the comic sense doesn't relate to his accent. In festivals where foreigners have watched the film, they have read the subtitle and laughed. That means it is the situation that is funny.

ME: The pace of the first and last third of the film is faster than the middle part. It seems the pace slows down in the middle. An example is the time between the two halves. In a way, we feel it is longer than the usual fifteen-minute break. Didn't you think you should add sub-plots for that part?

JP: I think we managed to hold the viewer's interest throughout. We reach a point when the audience can't take their eyes off the screen. So I was not worried about the audience. This slow pace starts with the toilet scene. And after that we see the scene of the girl and the soldier talking to each other. Because these two scenes are long and static, they may seem boring. However, the boy's suspicious search in the toilets somehow brings back the thrill element.

ME: I think that these scenes are dramatic and not boring. However, an example of slow pace is the scene of the girls designing the soccer match.

JP: That scene is almost ninety seconds and it features découpage in the style of TV reportage. I thought if we omitted this scene then we wouldn't get the girls' love for soccer.

ME: Interestingly, I feel the girls are not that much into soccer, and it is the flaw of the movie. It is always in arguments that we feel someone is into soccer, but that is not shown well. For instance, at the time of the Iran-Bahrain match, the main discussion was about whether Ali Daei[8] should be on the team or not. You could have used that. I can guess why you didn't use that kind of argument in the film. You were so obsessed with the main theme of the film and didn't want to disturb the harmonious feelings of the people towards the match. However, this is not the reality. When a number of soccer fans get together, their love for a team and also their approval or disapproval of a coach leads to heated discussions.

JP: Based on my experience, I think that when it is time for the national matches, even those fanatical fans try to restrain themselves and only support the national team.

ME: Let's say that in reality you are right; still you could have done it more dramatically.

JP: I believe if we had dug into it more than what we see, then we would have harmed the film. Maybe my experience of watching national matches led me to forget about discussions like that. I even had some shots with that kind of argument going on; in the bus scene we had hot discussions about the Persepolis and Esteghlal teams, but in the end I omitted all of it. Because it was not real. It was fabricated. And there are people who ask us how is it possible that even when detained, these girls only talk about soccer. We tried to stand in the middle.

ME: I think the difference between Iranian and foreign audiences of the film is clear in this instance. It is possible that in the eyes of a foreigner, the depiction of different aspects of soccer in the film is convincing, but I still feel it is not enough. If it hadn't been you, who are known for being a soccer lover, I would have doubted the director of *Offside*'s interest in this sport, from the way it is represented here.
JP: We had written different conversations about soccer, but then we felt that being detained is something that doesn't let these girls say what they really feel.

ME: I am not talking about the reflection of reality. I am talking about using these ideas as script materials. If we had fans talking about our league, then we would have more character development. I mean, through these discussions we could have guessed this person is a fan of Persepolis, this one loves Ali Karimi, and this is the one who adores Enayati.
JP: Maybe you are looking at it from a masculine point of view. For some girls, soccer is an excuse. They want to go to the stadium to see what this forbidden place looks like. Maybe they dawdle at home, in school or other places, but now that they are in the stadium, they are looking for something else.

ME: This is where we see it differently. I think soccer discussions could have changed them into characters. Right now, it feels as if these girls are part of the large majority of general soccer lovers, those for whom soccer is just an excuse. Maybe one of them should have been a fanatical soccer fan, a walking encyclopedia of soccer. In that way they would be characters, not prototypes.
JP: One of the découpage restrictions I made for myself was not to trespass on their privacy. As if I was saying the stadium belongs to men, and this small space belongs to women. And while women are not allowed to enter this place, men are not allowed to enter here, and we are between them. In order to keep this cinematic approach intact, I stuck to it until the end. If my camera had entered their private lives, then we would have learned more about their characters. But I didn't want to step into their ground. I wanted them to have their own ground and for men also to have their own. So we would stand outside both grounds and judge.

ME: In other words, *Offside* stands in the center of two axes. One axis is documentary film and the other is fiction. In a documentary there is no answer for the problem and you make the film to find the answer, but in a fiction film you have a presupposition and work on it and make your own world. *Offside* wants to use both the advantages of a documentary film and a fiction film. And standing in the middle has its own problems. For me as a viewer, the documentary features of the film are more interesting, like the scene where the camera follows the soldier in the crowd or the scene where the first girl enters the stadium or the ending celebration scene.

JP: Keeping the documentary feel of the film was more important for me. Though I was happy with the mise-en-scène of my previous films, here I distanced myself from that because I didn't want to lose the convincing feeling that the film was reaching.

ME: Did it ever occur to you what would happen if, during the course of making and screening the film, the problem of women going to the stadium were resolved?

JP: My aim in my last three films was to make a report, showing that we lived like this, in this period of time. But it is not mere reportage; it is mixed with artistic sensitivities. With this approach, it is not important what would happen in the real world. If something happens, my goal would not be shattered. If they don't let women into the stadium, it means the problem remains, and if they do let them in, then in the future, when the situation has changed, the movie says that at that time such a restriction existed. In my opinion this film has no expiration date, and future changes would not affect its documentary value. We are in the World Cup mood. Well, we wanted our movie to be screened before the World Cup because once it's over, we become fed up with soccer. However, when time goes by, it doesn't matter anymore.

ME: In recent years, there was lots of talk about films made for festivals, made for a specific kind of audience. Personally I disagree with this idea, and I believe it is possible for any movie to have audiences abroad without having much of an audience in Iran.

JP: We are living in an over-politicized society and it is very common to link any subject to our desired ideology. Cinema is not an exception. When on TV they talk about "festival films," everything goes through political filters. For example, they call a group of movies "commissioned films" or "politically motivated," and at the same time they praise Michael Moore because he has attacked the Bush presidency. Yet Americans never say Moore made this film for the sake of Iranian authorities and not for us. We say such things because we don't consider any international place for ourselves. There is this belief that these movies are made to make foreigners happy and that we should be sorry about it. When we say foreigners praised *The Circle,* it means filmmakers like Bernardo Bertolucci and Miloš Forman also praised it. Can we say they loved this film because they are enemies of Iran?

ME: If Japanese say that Kurosawa's films are not reflections of Japan's reality, can't we have our own independent relationship with his films? Maybe when we are living in a certain reality, that reality becomes very important for us, and this is natural. But when you are far from that reality, an indirect relationship develops between the audience and the work of art. Let's get back to the film. Something that really irritated me in the film was the main character's main motive for going to the stadium, which was her friend getting killed during the Iran-Japan soccer match.

JP: We have a motive for each one of the girls, but we didn't work that much on them. In the festive mood of the ending, when the audience realizes this, their feelings change drastically, and naturally it is more effective and bolder. And another thing is I wanted to pay my debt to these seven persons.

ME: But the moment in which this information is revealed poses a threat to the film, to the extent that audiences might think the movie is made only for the sake of this ending information.

JP: Exactly, we anticipated this. But we told ourselves the hell with the film critics who are going to say this moment is too sentimental!

ME: And the result was that *Cahiers du cinéma* called the film chauvinistic.

JP: I'll tell you why *Cahiers du cinéma* didn't understand the film. After the nuclear talks, they got sensitive regarding nationalism, because in their opinion, the result of nationalism is national, ethnic, and racial supremacy, and they think this collides with intellectualism. Nationalism in Iran now is a different narrative, different from what the government propagandizes. I see it as a renaissance. *Cahiers du cinéma* got the wrong impression about the kind of nationalism at work here. I selected the anthem that consists of only Persian words—it doesn't talk about any governmental system, and it talks about my country, its people and nature. I did it purposefully because I don't make my films for any festival or with certain audiences in mind. I have to be able to call it "my" film and only I must pay the price for it.

ME: What the foreigners didn't realize is that soccer is one of the few things that bring unity to Iranian society, especially between Iranians living in Iran and those living abroad. Since 1998, soccer is the only thing that has united us all.

JP: I also think in the international screenings of *Offside*, it will be mostly Iranians who will welcome the film. Because they will find things in the movie they are nostalgic for.

ME: What do you think about how festivals approach films made outside the Hollywood system? Do they prefer these films?
JP: I think right now Hollywood dominates cinema more than ever, and commercial movies are welcomed more than before, which is one of the reasons for the decline in Iranian cinema's reception outside our borders. Audiences don't have the patience to watch them.

ME: Don't you think one of the reasons could be an increase in production of alternative films that don't satisfy audiences anymore?
JP: Iranian cinema has its own special attractions. *Offside* sold out a week before its screenings. At the movie's opening at the festival, almost two thousand people watched it, and it sold out for the next screening as well.

ME: What about this film attracted the foreign audience? What was their reaction?
JP: Korean viewers laughed during the scene when the girl wept for her friend. I thought they didn't understand the subtitle, so I talked to the distributor and told him there might be a mistake. He said, "There is no mistake and the subtitle was correct." I asked him, then, why they were laughing, and he said, "Well, it is funny to see that someone died because of a soccer match" [laughs]. And at the Berlin Film Festival, in the scene where the girls disguised in men's clothes try to enter the stadium, the Iranians in the audience laughed, and the Germans were looking at them surprised. That is why you cannot predict what the reaction will be. Shadmehr and I made a list of who laughs when! The main question for me is what the reaction will be of the audience here in Iran, of the people who are my real audience. I really like to sit with an Iranian audience at a public screening and watch the film.

ME: I think *Offside* is a film to be seen at the cinema. When you watch a movie with an audience the reactions are multiplied.
JP: Of course, especially when a good copy with good sound is screened.

ME: It is like watching a comedy film in a movie theater: When you watch it with other people you laugh more than when you watch it alone, and you ask yourself, why did I laugh in the cinema?
JP: When there are so many people watching a film, the first person who laughs makes others react and ask themselves, "Why am I restraining myself? Let's laugh and free ourselves!"

Notes

1. Renowned Iranian sports commentator and journalist, who passed away in 2017.
2. John Huston's 1981 film about POWs preparing for a soccer match against Nazi Germany's national team.
3. Iranian National Television broadcasts sporting matches with a brief delay in order to censor any "inappropriate" images whenever the camera captures the audience. This usually means replacing any shots of women in the audience with aerial shots from the match.
4. In English, *Bridge*.
5. Co-screenwriter, along with Panahi.
6. A neighborhood in Tehran.
7. One of two cinematographers on the shoot.
8. Iranian soccer superstar, now coach.

Report to History:
A Conversation with Jafar Panahi

Massoud Mehrabi[1] / 2006

From *Film International* 12.4 (Summer 2006): 42–51. Translated by Iante Roach.
Reprinted by permission.

Jafar Panahi, born in Mianeh, Iran in 1960, gained international recognition and won many prizes with his first feature film, *The White Balloon* (1995). His second film, *The Mirror* (1997), was not as successful, but the director attracted even greater international attention with *The Circle* (2000) and *Crimson Gold* (2003). His latest film, *Offside* (2006), earned the Silver Bear at the Berlin Film Festival. In this film Panahi deals with the ban on female spectators from sport stadiums in Iran. He narrates the story of a group of girls who are obliged to disguise themselves as boys in order to attend the Iran versus Bahrain international qualifying match for the 2006 FIFA World Cup.

Massoud Mehrabi: How were you attracted to cinema in the first place?
Jafar Panahi: Many years ago, when I was ten or twelve years old, I wrote a short story that won the first prize at our local library. At the time various amateur filmmakers were making 8mm films at Kanoon, the Institute for the Intellectual Development of Children and Young Adults.[2] They asked me to act in one of their films, only because they needed a fat actor! Moreover, a short story I had written and the prize I won for it had attracted some attention. So my first job in film was acting in an 8mm film called *The Elephant and the Teacup*. A thin boy and I played a game called *gillidanda*.[3] Depending on which one of us managed to knock a small stick further away, the other one would have to give him a piggyback ride. When I had to carry the thin boy piggyback, everything went well, but when he lost the game, trouble broke out! He had to look for a solution to be able to carry me, heavy as I was. So he kept looking this way and that, and in the end arrived at a building site full of workers who had a handcart. He lifted me onto it and the problem was

solved. The film was five or six minutes long. Then I worked on various films as an assistant director.

My father, who painted buildings for a living, played a very important role in encouraging me. Later I bought a still camera and started working with it. I took photographs and exhibited them until I began military service, and then I continued taking photographs, but on the war's front lines. I even held an exhibition at the garrison. A television director visited one of my photography exhibitions in Marivan and offered me a job. He wanted me to produce radio reports from the war front. I refused to do that, but I offered to do video reports with my old 8mm camera instead. In the end they agreed and posted me to the region's national television center in Sanandaj.

MM: So this is how you began working as a cameraman with old 16mm cameras that had three lenses: tele, wide, and normal?

JP: Yes. And since there was also a darkroom there, I could make my film appear quickly and see the results of my work. These documentary-reportage films were mostly broadcast in Iranian Kurdistan. Later I filmed various military operations, side by side with soldiers who had been my companions during military service. They had weapons and I had my camera. One action I filmed was the Mohammad Rasulullah operation.[4] I also edited the documentary film I made about it, a twenty-two or twenty-three-minute long film that was broadcast by Iran's national television.

MM: Was this when you also learned film editing?

JP: I actually began editing films when I started working with my 8mm camera. It was mainly for fun, and one of my friends who worked in television in Kurdistan helped me a great deal. I had finished my military service by the time I was working at that television station. Then I took the national university entrance exam and was accepted.

MM: Where were you accepted?

JP: I was accepted into the College of Cinema and TV in 1984. We were sixty students to start with, and our fields of specialization were determined during the following terms, with seven students directing, seven screenwriting, and so on. At the time, Kambuzia Partovi was shooting his film *The Fish.* I went on set and became one of his assistants. I had already made a 16mm, thirty-minute-long, behind-the-scenes documentary about his film *Golnar* (1988) as part of my research project at university. I called the documentary *The Second Look.* It was about the marionettes that Partovi used in the film.

MM: What did you do once university was over?

JP: After finishing university, I chose to be posted to the Bandar Abbas national television center and worked on four or five films there. I made films such as *The Friend* and *The Final Exam*, which won eight or nine awards at the first National Television Festival, dedicated exclusively to television films made in the provinces. At the time of the festival, I was working as assistant director to Abbas Kiarostami on *Through the Olive Trees*.

MM: It appears that you became assistant director on *Through the Olive Trees* in a very straightforward way, almost by chance.

JP: Yes, one day I called up Kiarostami and left a voice message saying that I had just graduated from the cinema faculty, was working in television, loved his films, and that I would love to work with him on his new film. Luckily for me, his team was not yet complete, so everything went ahead easily. I went on set on the first few days of the film shoot. I got down from a minibus and introduced myself. After two or three days of work, I became his first assistant director.

MM: What did you learn from working with Kiarostami? Were you attracted by his way of looking at cinema, or by the technical aspects and his way of making films?

JP: I had already experienced working as assistant director through my work with Kambuzia Partovi. The way Partovi worked with actors, for instance, has been important for me. But Kiarostami worked with actors in a different way. Because he found in real life the exact character types he wanted to film, there was not much need to work on acting. The most important aspect of Kiarostami's cinema was his precision and obsession with the image, in a way that previously I had only seldom seen. The images of his films, though relying on the script, were a separate language. At the time I was captivated by this sort of obsession and attention to detail. When I started doing my own films, my own methodology was different, for instance as regards working with actors, but Kiarostami's outlook and mindset certainly influenced my work. For example, now when I shoot a film I might even act out a scene for an actor and say, "This is the kind of acting I'm looking for," but I certainly undertake thorough searches to find my actors, to find actors with the right physical appearance.

MM: So, you don't start filming until you find the actors you're looking for, who must be perfectly suitable for their role, just as obsessively as Kiarostami?

JP: Not in such an unconditional way, no. Kiarostami's attention to images is the aspect of his work that truly influenced me. Understanding that images are even more important than the script. To the extent that at times images speak by themselves and shape the script. For instance, when working with Mr. Partovi, one day I realized that he had gotten his actors and the camera ready, but had not told the cameraman where to place the camera. When I asked him why, he said: "It doesn't matter, this is the story of two children, and the camera can be anywhere." Well, this was Partovi's view at the time. But Kiarostami's work was totally different. I remember an interesting aspect of working with him. Once he wanted to show me a new location for the first time, so he tied a scarf around my eyes when we were in the car one kilometer away from it. Once we got there, he took me by the hand and made me walk. He uncovered my eyes only when I was standing exactly where the camera would be, and I saw the prairie of the last shot of *Through the Olive Trees*. It is a stunning shot, not easy to achieve. Kiarostami certainly undertook many trips in order to find the exact location. The camera always had its own, very special physical location during his film shoots. It was placed in such a way that it would capture the real life of the film's characters.

MM: Your first film, *The White Balloon*, is still powerfully present in the minds of Iranian and foreign spectators after all these years. In people's consciousness, the film's title evokes your name. How did you make the film, which pays homage to Kiarostami's films of the period? Kiarostami wrote the script, but we can see interesting streaks of your own independent way of making films in it.

JP: During my university studies, I worked in the faculty's film archive and therefore saw many films. I remember that at the time I was a great fan of Hitchcock and saw all of his films and knew their storyboards, pace and editing very well. Before making *The White Balloon*, I had also made short films and documentaries in Bandar Abbas, as well as doing all the things I mentioned earlier. So while the script of *The White Balloon* was written by Kiarostami, the film was original. I think this has to do with the pace and editing that I had learned from Hitchcock and from Italian neorealism. I tried to make use of all these influences in my first film. The editing and the way I worked with the actors was also innovative. When I was making the film I kept thinking that my university professors were waiting to see the result. It felt as if I was about to take an exam.

MM: Even you could not have predicted the international success of *The White Balloon*. Why do you think the film was such a sensation?

JP: I have never tried to analyze that period to understand why this happened. From *The White Balloon* onwards, cinema became the principal thing in my life. I wanted to continue the path I had begun in the right way. I know very well that gaining success is hard, but continuing to be successful once you have gained success is even harder. So I had to think of a new way of making films, because I understood that if I stuck to a single methodology I would be repeating myself very soon. I was looking for new forms of cinematic expression and I think *The Mirror* was the result of these musings.

MM: But *The Mirror* was not as successful as *The White Balloon*.
JP: Perhaps because it was a sort of bridge between *The White Balloon* and *The Circle*.

MM: We will get to *The Circle*. But why do you think not as successful as *The White Balloon*, despite continuing the same artistic journey?
JP: It is always like this. If you look at the filmographies of ninety percent of filmmakers all over the world who made a first successful film, you will see that they were not able to maintain the same level of success with their subsequent films. In *The Mirror* I was after a new way of looking and a new form of expression. Halfway through the film, everything suddenly changes and we see something new take shape. If the film had continued in the same vein as the first half, it might have been more popular. The way I saw it, I was living in a society where people have developed two separate personalities. When we go to the office, some people pretend to be someone they are not, and then behave differently once in private.

MM: You changed direction halfway through *The Mirror* because you truly understood this issue?
JP: I tried to express the content of the film through its form, which led to my splitting the film into two parts. The first part is the film that I started making, and the second part is the reality created by the principal character, the little girl. It was still me who made this second part of the film, but in any case I wanted to say that people with two personalities live at the heart of our society. This is why I chose this form. It might seem rough and rudimentary, but it was an experiment. Maybe this is why *The Mirror* did not have the same outlook as my first film, and was not as successful. In *The White Balloon*, I recounted the narrative in a classical way. In *The Mirror* instead I broke the rules and made an experimental film. Of course if I hadn't made *The Mirror* I would not have made *The Circle*. Only after having made one, I found the courage to make the other. I wanted the film's content, the plot, to be in service to the film's form and thereby depart from classical filmmaking. This required putting aside all I had learned from Hitchcock's films and from the many others I had watched if only to show that I wanted to make films in a different way. I did not insert the credit "a film by Jafar Panahi" in the closing titles of *The White Balloon* or *The Mirror*, because I thought that I had yet to make my first film. These two films were like homework, dress rehearsals, for the film I had in mind and really wanted to make. With *The Circle*, the credit appears for the first time. My first film is *The Circle*.

MM: From *The Circle* onwards, you have been making semi-journalistic films. Your films do not deal with causes, but rather with effects. Considering that you started out with the delicate, poetic, and eternal narrative of *The White Balloon*, how did you arrive at such radical, manifesto-like subjects in your following films?

JP: When you work with children in cinema, and with children in general, their very presence brings a delicate gaze with it. When you look at the world from their perspective, even if you are going to address social issues, these acquire an altogether childlike quality. And unconsciously you do not see the violence of the adult world. On the other hand, I was always interested in social issues. Perhaps also because I lived in areas where people had social and financial problems, which I saw very closely. This world that I knew certainly had an impact on my last three films. On the other hand, I always thought that I had certain responsibilities, such as reporting the conditions of where and how I've lived, for the sake of history.

This interest in "historical reports" began at university. At the time, I made a documentary called *Yarali Bashar* about *Qama Zani* and dedicated it "To History" in the opening titles. I imagined at the time that twenty or thirty years later we would have this document recording this ceremony. The film shows a small "excerpt" of the events of that period. Perhaps the journalistic outlook that you mentioned derives from this feeling of social responsibility that's long been a part of my nature. All three of my films *The Circle*, *Crimson Gold*, and *Offside* report on aspects of social history. They deal chiefly with social issues and the restrictions we face on a day-to-day basis.

MM: *Crimson Gold* is in some ways a continuation of *The Circle*. The latter presents poverty and prostitution, and a reflection on the milieu that abuses women. In *Crimson Gold*, you tackle social differences and the divide between the rich and the poor, a crucial issue in contemporary Iran. How did you develop such continuity in your outlook?

JP: After *The Circle*, my train of thought was clear. From this point on, I wanted to make films about restrictions, which could include anything, from women's problems to social differences and divisions. All these are suitable film topics. In *The Circle*, I tackled the issues of women and prostitutes, which can also have financial roots. This is especially the case because we live in a society in which, for various reasons, financial matters do not follow their natural course. A very small sector of society has become unnaturally wealthy while the poorest social class has widened exponentially, and meanwhile the middle class is disappearing. Well, how can this have happened? It has been caused by people who did not gain their wealth in a regular way, and who are unable to use their wealth to create work. This has a negative impact on the lower classes, the combination of all these factors leads to corruption, and the social divide gradually increases. Social divisions exist all over the world, but in many places social classes have maintained their identity. There is an upper class, a lower class, and a middle class. They cooperate in a productive way or at any rate coexist side by side despite their differences and difficulties. But here in Iran, both the lower and middle classes are being sacrificed. In *Crimson Gold* Hussein belongs to the lower class, which is gradually disappearing in relevance. Nobody takes notice of him.

MM: As a consequence of its "journalistic aspect," the film deals with appearances and superficiality. As an Iranian, of course I know what you are saying. But for future generations and people who do not live in Iran, the reasons for this may not be clear. Both in *The Circle* and in *Crimson Gold* we see this external layer of society, but we do not see the causes of the situation.

JP: I thought that both showing and explaining them would be excessive.

MM: I'm not suggesting you explain. I'm talking about semiotics, about signs that can acquaint us at least symbolically with the roots of the situation.

JP: If we look at the films in the way that you just described, we can see various sorts of signs. When the character who lives in the huge building block in *Crimson Gold* recounts how his father built it and talks about how he makes his living, all these minor details illuminate the heart of the matter. I really believe that additional hints would be superfluous and didactic. Imagine if we gave further information on each character in *The Circle*. It would block the thought process and creativity of the audience. I think these films are like a spark that must enter the minds of the spectators. On the basis of their knowledge, awareness, and world-view, all these combined with what the film has to say, the spectators are forced to think. I do not know if it is my duty to show where the roots of the problems lie and how they can be solved, or not. I certainly do not believe that films have the responsibility to solve problems. At any rate, the signs you mention are present in various instances throughout the film. I did not emphasize them deliberately. I wanted to give the audience the chance to get to the heart of the matter and to reach the same interpretation I arrived at.

MM: In *Offside* we encounter a more unusual theme compared to those found in *The Circle* and *Crimson Gold*. A more specific topic, having to do with women. How did you think of it, and why did you want to make the film? Only because women are not allowed to enter football stadiums, or in order to tackle greater issues?

JP: In *Offside*, we are once again confronted with the issue of restrictions—the difficulties that exist for a specific gender unable to progress alongside the other gender. This was the basis of the film. I was wondering how I could craft a story dealing with this special subject.

In my youth I adored football and goalkeeping, and I used to go to football matches in stadiums, so I knew the background of the subject very well. When the team returned to Iran, my wife, son, daughter, and I went to Azadi Stadium to celebrate. When we got there, the stadium was filled with fans and they weren't letting anyone in. We were told that 5,000 women had suddenly attacked and entered the stadium, so that the people in charge were especially not letting any more women in. This was the first spark, and its image stuck in my mind. On a couple of occasions, I went to the stadium with my daughter, who adores football, to see the training sessions of the national team up close. I told my wife to come with us so that she could take our daughter back home if she wasn't allowed in. It was natural that they should not let her in, but my daughter said, "I'm coming anyway!" and after ten minutes there she was, next to me. I did not understand what trick she had played, but, well, this was another spark for me. And the last spark was the penultimate qualifying match of 2006, which almost qualified Iran for the World Cup series. I realized that the time had come to make the film.

MM: A few good films, both documentary and fiction, have been made about the last time that Iran did take part in the World Cup in 1998. Did these films have any influence on how the plot took shape in your mind?

JP: I remember one of the films, by Ebrahim Asgharzadeh. It did not tackle the question of women entering stadiums, but of course all of these films influenced me to some extent.

MM: In your previous films you had complete control of the set. But in *Offside* you had to improvise more. Did you plan in advance how to shoot on location for those scenes that can only take place once, both before and after the match?

JP: My experience working in television as well as filming on the front lines in the war helped me overcome the difficulties of this film. And of course, I went on set with a plan ready. I knew what I wanted to film at the start, middle, and end of the match, and which images would be of use for the film. Since I am well-versed in editing, I was storyboarding and editing simultaneously and, in my head, understanding which scenes I needed to place next to each other. At times the shoot went ahead just as we wanted, and at times it didn't. So then we would set up the scene again the way we had to have it and bring the film forward. I knew what I had to do in between the start and the end of the shoot. For instance, I knew that the father had to enter the stadium and look for his daughter, but I didn't know what the real conclusion of the film would be. I remember sitting down in the stadium during the game, together with the director of photography Mahmoud Kalari and my other colleagues, whilst other members of the film's team were stationed in

Vanak Square and wondering together with them what would happen if Iran lost the game. Naturally had this been the case, the film would have had to end in a different way. But thanks to our getting our desired outcome, it was as if we had scripted the game and it went ahead according to plan.

MM: So you had only written the first half of the script before the shoot began, rather than a full script?
JP: Of course we had a full script, but it changed from day to day. Each film shoot went ahead according to the events of the day. For instance, the scenes riding around town in the minibus were added later.

MM: Both in *The Circle* and in *Crimson Gold* you chose actors that correspond to real people one can see in Iran. How did you choose the actresses of *Offside*?
JP: You have to consider that these girls came to the shoot disguised as boys in order to play their roles. They are somewhat different from the characters of my other films, in which actors played characters of the same social background, who had experienced the same difficulties. But in *Offside* these girls want to reach their goals by pretending to be someone else. The girls belong to different social classes and have their own counterparts in real life. If we look for these girls in the world around us we will find them very easily.

MM: Did you make *Offside* in order to solve a social problem?
JP: Naturally my first aim was to create a historical report. My previous films and now *Offside* fulfill this. And then I wanted to find a solution for the issue. Of course what really bothered me was feeling that we have all become distant from each other in the lives we lead. In the film I show that once the game starts and all the events slowly unfold, every single character, from the girls to the soldiers, gradually becomes closer to the others. In the end they all participate in a national celebration side by side, thanks to their love for their nation. Now, returning to the world outside the film, just as I said, we are all distant from each other and scattered all over the place. We need an exciting motivation to gather together. Maybe this is why at the end of the film they all had no choice but to get together, whether they wanted to or not. My inner voice tells me that this film might be able to open the way for women being allowed into stadiums. This is part of the reason I insist on its release in Iran.

MM: Some of the girls in the film play character types who do not exist in our society. Especially one of them, whom I think ordinary Iranian spectators would not find believable. The ignorant girl who speaks like a villain. Similar characters, whether men or women, would not even be allowed into English stadiums. Why didn't you choose a character typology closer to Iranian women instead of this lumpen and feisty girl—though, of course, from a cinematic point of view she is interesting and fun—in order to help solve the issue of women who want to go and watch football?

JP: First of all, you must consider that ninety percent of stadium-goers in Iran are young, from the age of twelve on up. Then there are those older folk who really loved football in their youth. Even though they are now married and have other problems, they still take these matches very seriously. Secondly, die-hard football fans at football matches are a specific personality type all over the world. The way they look and speak is very different to the world outside the stadium. Especially in Iran ever since the revolution, with the absence of women, the atmosphere of stadiums has become totally masculine. The fans perceive themselves as being free and speak openly. I have heard them utter vulgarities in stadiums many times, and told myself that I would have been ashamed had my son been there with me. The actors I chose for this film are exactly like the girl that you remember as being "lumpen." Perhaps the absence of such people in this context is what would raise questions. That girl is exactly the sort of person you would find in a stadium. She dressed herself up this way in order to attract less attention. Actually, she is the person who aroused the least suspicion in the whole group. Even the police struggled to recognize her as a girl. Moreover, I don't think that every film about women should represent all women in society. People go to the stadium because they love football. Now, a few girls dressed themselves up in that way and I thought theirs was the right decision. I could have made the film come very close to reality, but I wanted to manipulate reality a little. If you really want to portray reality, it would be very difficult to recognize girls in that group. My maneuvers had to do with the fact that I wanted to show our football fans as civilized people. For instance, when the boys help the girls to escape in the toilet scene. I wanted to say that our male football fans are so intelligent and civilized that they tolerate the presence of female football fans beside them.

MM: Once the film is released and Iranian families watch it, how do you think they will react to the girls? Do you think they will empathize with them?

JP: Yes, and this was the case at Fajr Film Festival. I passed by all the theatres where the nine or ten festival screenings of the film took place, from the press screening to theatres where ordinary spectators were watching it. I saw extraordinarily positive reactions and absolutely felt the empathy that you mention. If Iranian spectators are the intended audience, then the answer was positive. And the sales office of the distributors of *Offside* received many demonstrations of interest the day after the first screening.

MM: In both *Crimson Gold* and *The Circle* you tackle taboos that make it difficult for the films to be released for the general public. Some people believe that this is a deliberate choice of yours.

JP: Well, we know what kind of society we live in and what issues we face. I always have a strong motivation to make a film, because if I started thinking of the problems at the outset I would be bound to self-censor myself to some extent, and this would damage the film. If I make a film against my own wishes, it is no longer my own film, and this means I have been lying to myself. No, I really do not think about these issues. For me the most important matter is making the film, a difficult process in itself. If I thought about the difficulties, the film would not even begin. The next stage is having to accept the reality of film screenings. I need to stand by my word and not remove a single shot from any film I make, even if that means it won't play in Iranian theatres. Because in that case it will enter the market by way of CDs and DVDs. Do you know anyone in Iran who has not seen *The Circle?* The same now applies to *Offside.*

MM: Well, do you make your films for the Iranian audience or not?
JP: No, I make my films for myself.

MM: How important to you are developments in Iranian cinema and getting your films screened and released in Iranian theatres?
JP: Well, it depends on two stages. The first is the stage before I make the film, during which time nothing matters to me—not the audience, not the opinions of critics or festivals, not the film's chances of getting a wide release. What matters at this point is that I want to make a film and so need to start envisioning its production. The second stage takes place after the film shoot, when I ask myself whether the film will be seen or not. And if not, of what use will the film be? How is it possible to make a film that will not be released in a regular manner and that will not be seen by Iranian audiences? And if the film does not have a financial return, how will I make my next film? I trained myself to avoid self-censorship during the first stage by not thinking about these matters, so I am at peace with all of this. So far, I have made four films and I am proud that *Offside* is my fifth. I comfort myself thinking that these few films were all films I really wanted to make.

MM: Is this why you edit your own films? Is the reasoning behind this choice the fact that you are making the film for yourself?
JP: I don't know. I would have liked someone else to edit *The White Balloon.* Looking back, I realize that I loved editing from the time I did 8mm films, and that I edited most of my friends' films before doing military service. When we finished shooting *The White Balloon* everything was set for me to start working with an

editor. But when he saw the film, I really didn't like the first few things he said. This is why I never gave my films to an editor again, to avoid having someone else's taste imposed on my films.

MM: The twenty minutes following the first hour of *Offside* feel a little long. Perhaps the pace of this part of the film would have worked better had it been edited by someone else.

JP: Unlike my previous films that open with a punch in the stomach, *Offside* begins with a slow pace and then gradually ropes in the viewer. No, I don't think any section of the film is too long, or that spectators might get bored. The subtle hints that I inserted throughout the film prevent the audience from getting bored. I made the length of the film coincide with the 90 minutes of a football match.

MM: Do you produce your own films in order to prevent others from imposing their tastes on you?

JP: Yes, and this too has to do with difficulties that exist in this country. If the film is produced by someone other than me, this person might create problems for me. If a producer tells me to shorten a part of the film, I can resist and insist. And if I work with a producer who also produces films by other directors, this might create difficulties for his or her future films. And then I would feel guilty for having caused him or her damage. If I produce my own films, I do not encounter these difficulties.

MM: What do you think about Iran's commercial cinema?

JP: I think the cinema industry of every country needs all sorts of films to be made, artistic and commercial, and actually the two complement one another. Commercial films can reach a wider audience and thus generate enough revenue to sustain the industry. On the other hand, art films can raise the overall quality of cinema. As I said, the two complement one another. The second issue is that we have all sorts of films in Iran and must understand what kind of films the audience wants to see. This way we can respect the audience. I believe that in *Offside* both aspects are present. The film satisfies both ordinary and intellectual spectators.

MM: In Iran you and other filmmakers are considered to be making festival films, films intended for foreign audiences.

JP: Whatever you do in this society, they create a problem for you. And every success you gain is followed by problems. When I made *The White Balloon* and it gained recognition, someone asked me how much money I'd won thanks to film prizes. I said: "Sixty-thousand dollars." Their reply was: "Poor you, you have just made yourself sixty-thousand enemies." When I was shooting *The Mirror*, a film critic passed by the set just as I was filming the first shot and realized that I was making my second film. He said: "Make whatever film you want to make, I have already written my review!" So, this problem exists. If you appear on the scene, you automatically attract attention and you can easily be accused of anything. I put my finger on social problems, and this always causes me trouble.

MM: The kind of films you make are considered niche, art films all over the world and do not have a wide audience. As a producer, how well do your films get distributed and do their financial returns enable you to make new films?

JP: I make a film every three years or so, but I could probably make two studio films per year, including Iranian blockbusters. But the truth is that before I make a film my only concern is whether I love the project or not. If my answer is yes, I put my whole life at its service. Whether the film will break even or not is a secondary concern for me. Now that I'm internationally known and my films are highly respected, naturally producers want to work and secure contracts with me. I usually start filming and then halfway through the shoot I get co-producers on board. This way, I get the money to make the film and am able to finish it peacefully. So far, using this method, my films have not made financial losses. I am not worried about finding producers in Iran and abroad.

MM: You are right to say that first of all you make films for yourself, but yours is usually a foreign audience.

JP: This happened in an unsolicited way.

MM: Don't you think that this might cause your future films to have a foreign flavor?

JP: If I was only concerned with festivals, I would never have made *Offside,* a film intended for a wider audience.

MM: At any rate, foreign audiences, with their tastes and outlook, do have an influence on your films, you cannot hide this.

JP: I cannot give you a detailed answer. Whether consciously or unconsciously, we all love being encouraged and appreciated. But I'd also say with confidence that clarity of vision and love of cinema guide my filmmaking more than any outside influences. For instance, when *The White Balloon* was released Mr. Kiarostami was asked to write something about my work, and wrote, "Considering Panahi's love for cinema and his deep understanding of images, it is impossible for him to make a bad film." I am completely in love with cinema, in a pure way. More than anything, cinema constitutes my world. And I have nothing to hide on this score: I'm proud of the success my films have achieved abroad. I climbed up the steps of any festival you can imagine and gained their top awards. Yet I am not content to find a formula for success and repeat it. If I were, I'd have kept making movies like my first hit, *The White Balloon*. I understood that I needed a new experience, and this is why I try to vary my films with each one. I'm happy to show my work wherever I can, but my chief concern after finishing a film is whether I can present it in my own country or not. I experienced my happiest moment last year, when *Offside* was presented at the Fajr Film Festival.

MM: What are your next plans?

JP: I really don't know what's going to happen next. After finishing both *The Circle* and *Crimson Gold* I thought I might not make films again. In any case, the three-year process must run its course. And of course I have many scripts ready, for instance an historical film about Hassan-i Sabbah,[5] set one thousand years ago, that I really want to make. But I am not yet sure whether this must be my sixth film. It has to remain with me long enough that I start feeling I must make this film.

MM: Do you think you might work with professional actors in your next films?

JP: It is not unlikely. It depends on the subject and film style.

MM: Good luck!

JP: Thank you.

Notes

1. Film critic and owner of *Film Monthly* (Tehran), in which most of Panahi's Iranian interviews have appeared.
2. An Iranian institution, founded in 1965 and still operating a wide range of cultural and artistic activities for children and young adults, including libraries, publishing children's books and sound recordings, and theatrical and film production.
3. An ancient street game played primarily in rural parts of Central and South Asia.
4. The 27th Mohammad Rasulullah Brigade was established in Tehran during the Iran–Iraq War and did most of its operations in the southern part of Iran.
5. Hassan-i Sabbah (circa 1050–1124) was the leader of the Nizari Ismailites and the founder of the order known as Assassins.

Offside Rules:
An Interview with Jafar Panahi

Maryam Maruf / 2006

From *openDemocracy.net,* June 7, 2006. Reprinted by permission.

In just a few days' time, on June 11, Iran officially begins its 2006 German World Cup adventure. If they triumph and proceed to the knockout stages, the Iranian president, Mahmoud Ahmadinejad himself, has suggested that he would show his support by coming over and watching them play live—a move which has been cautiously frowned upon by German Chancellor Angela Merkel. Would Ahmadinejad be banned from attending the World Cup?

Soccer, as the clichés go, is a controversial thing—a game of two halves no less—and the subject of Jafar Panahi's brilliant new film, *Offside.* Inspired by the occasion when his own daughter was refused entry to a football stadium, *Offside* isn't really about football, but rather what happens when a group of six girls try to sneak into that sacred space—the stadium where the Iran-Bahrain World Cup qualifying match is taking place. According to a law "passed" after the 1979 Islamic revolution, women are forbidden from watching live soccer matches, a decision which Ahmadinejad wished to repeal but was overruled by the *ulema.*

The girls are caught, and though excluded from the game, they are not allowed to go home. So while Iran's most important match in years unfolds within earshot but out of view, they are put in the custody of three young, bewildered but traditional-minded army conscripts. United by their patriotism ("What, so my problem is that I was born in Iran?") and obsessive desire for Iran to win, but divided by their views on the proper place for women, the characters in *Offside* represent a society that is in the process of tumultuous and unregulated change.

The film, shot like a documentary and using nonprofessional actors, is just under ninety-minutes long and structured in a similar manner to a match. Full of small, comic incidents and surprising moments, the audience suffers the same agony as the characters: will Iran qualify for the world cup? But of course much more is at stake, and with a dull undercurrent of fear, you wonder, what punishment does "the Chief" have in store for the captured girls?

• • •

Maryam Maruf: How did you go about making the film inside Iran? An article in *Time* says you submitted a phony synopsis to the authorities who later found out they were duped. I felt as I was watching the film that something awful was going to happen (I was at points reminded of Siddiq Barmak's *Osama*). Did you and your crew feel that too when you were working? Did you expect the police to pounce at any minute?

Jafar Panahi: Many things in Iran always have certain problems. For each film that we make we have to think of creative ways of doing it. In Farsi we have a saying: "If you can't get through the door, then climb up through the window." So this is what we have to do to find a way of achieving our aims. For each film this method can only be used once, and for the next one obviously we have to find an alternative way of doing it.

We gave a script to the authorities and it was slightly different—we said that it was just about some boys who go to a football match. Once they approved that film, we went about making *this* film. We didn't have any problems with the police, but the Ministry of Culture and Islamic Guidance—the organization that approves film releases—told us that it would not give us a license because it was not happy with my previous films. It said that I must amend them according to its wishes, and only then would it give me a license to release this film—and it said that this would take at least a year. Well, time was passing and I wanted to have the film out before the World Cup, so we just went ahead and produced the film.

MM: Are men in Iran generally sympathetic to the women's interest in attending matches or do they mostly feel that stadiums are a masculine preserve?

JP: Before the revolution women were allowed to attend football matches, the same as men, and the current restrictions came only after the revolution in 1979. Because of this kind of ideology, the mentality of the people has changed, and so it is this "official" mentality that is causing all the problems. But in my opinion, the majority of men do not have a problem with women attending matches. But since women were banned from attending, the whole atmosphere of the matches became very male and chauvinistic and rude, and it has by now developed its own momentum.

MM: How often do girls and women actually get into legal trouble for sneaking into matches, as opposed to being turned away and sent home?

JP: The same thing happens to women who don't observe the *hijab* properly; it is what you call "bad *hijab*" when they show some of their hair. The vice squad are sent to deal with them. The women are fined, or they are sometimes detained and imprisoned, or their families are sent for and they have to guarantee that they will not behave like this again. So this is how it is done. But again, it is all about the way that the authorities interpret the laws.

MM: Can you expand on the idea of the murkiness of the women and football issue: what's really banned, who does the banning? And can you comment on the interpretation of the law on various levels—civil and religious authorities, soldiers and police?

JP: Of course, when you try to restrict something or implement a restriction, it has to be based on some sort of law. But there is nothing in the law that has been approved by the Iranian parliament or anybody else that bans women from taking part. It has become a kind of unwritten law. The policemen and the soldiers too, have to follow this unwritten law and unwritten rules, and they are answerable to their superiors for it.

MM: Stylistically, the film is very much like a documentary. You use nonprofessional actors and events unfold in real time—there is even a half-time toilet break!

JP: Yes, all the actors are nonprofessionals. The film is constructed like a documentary in which I have inserted fictional characters. Are we in a documentary, or is this fiction? I wanted the action to reflect this ambiguity. We tried to preserve a unity of time, so with each second that passes, I want the audience to feel that they are watching a real event unfold. The places are real, the event is real, and so are the characters and the extras. This is why I purposefully chose not to use professional actors, as their presence would have introduced a notion of falseness.

MM: Where did you find the actors? Were the girls in reality football fans who were sympathetic to the storyline?

JP: When I write a script I look around for people who can do the job best. For example, the soldier I found in Tabriz, in the northwest of Iran. For the girls, they were mainly university students—and I found them through friends and colleagues and my contacts at universities. As far as their interest in football, yes, they are genuinely interested and passionate about football. They wanted to go to the matches.

Fortunately in Iran the actors or actresses do not get into trouble. The main problem is for the producers and directors. Of course, I've gotten into trouble in the past, so I don't mind so much—and I'm used to it—but as far as the actors are concerned, there was no danger to them.

MM: The film is very funny, and at times almost farcical. How important is humor to you in telling the story?

JP: I believe that it is the greatest insult to women that they have to deny their identity as women and have to dress as men to take part in society. So yes, there is humor, but it is bitter humor. You may laugh at it, but nevertheless you feel very sad that women have to deny their femininity to take part in a function where men can take part.

In the film I have deliberately included a female character who wears the *chador*. By that I want to show that it is not only people who are not religious and outside this group that have problems, but that even a religious person—who is prepared to wear the *hijab*—is restricted and not allowed to take part. The authorities are being unfair to the religious people as well as the nonreligious people—both simply want to watch a game, or take part in male functions, and both are being marginalized and deprived.

Restrictions are imposed throughout different strata and classes of people. My aim in bringing together people from different classes and religious backgrounds is to show that everybody is subject to these sorts of restrictions and laws.

The reason given by people who say women should not go to these matches is the rowdy language, the curses and the swearing; they feel that ladies should not be exposed to that behavior. But another point made by the *ulema* recently (in connection with the latest rulings) is that it is not correct for women to go there and see men with bare arms and legs. So even if they don't derive any enjoyment from it the very fact of seeing men in that position is considered to be bad. This adds a further argument for exclusion of women.

MM: The element of masquerade and disguise is very important in *Offside* and also in films such as *Marmoulak*.¹ Is this inherent ingenuity what scares the authorities so much?

JP: This element of masquerade is a general characteristic of all the films made in Iran. They have different layers of meaning and messages. This is what annoys the authorities—and the same thing is true for television, which in Iran is wholly state-owned. So it's not just that the authorities don't like the message, they don't even want to have the questions raised in the first place. The very raising of the issue of women and their status in society and their desire to go to a football match—this is something that challenges the authorities, and they don't have the sufficient strength of character or tolerance to handle it.

The Iranian regime is a religious regime and there are many religious controls, but these ideas are limited to those who are in power and how they interpret religion. Even among the clerics there are some very enlightened people who do not believe in these sorts of exclusions, but unfortunately they are outside the sphere of power and although they want to open up, those who are inside have a much narrower reading of religious ideas. This is what causes the problem.

We are not trying to fight against anybody or challenge anybody with our films. All we want to do is raise a social issue. We want to tell those in government that there is this problem so at least they can think more deeply about it. We want to persuade them that there are more rational ways of tackling and dealing with these problems than sheer restriction or ignoring them.

MM: Patriotism, duty, and honor are major themes, and it was interesting that you explored this through the younger generation.

JP: This is a good question and an important point. When you are talking about nationalism and patriotism, we have to realize that this is not about chauvinism or the superiority of one race or country. Ever since the revolutionary regime came to power, it has fought against some inherited national traditions like *Nowruz*.

People in Iran want to return to their national identity. They want to say that they have a long history and that there are many points of pride in that long history. They want to reclaim their traditions and to say that we are a cultured people, and we can live together under those shared cultural values.

Notes

1. Kamal Tabrizi's *The Lizard* (2004).

A Response to Ahmad Talebinejad's Letter: None of My People Reaches Old Age

Jafar Panahi / 2006

From *Film Monthly* (Tehran) 24.350 (August 2006): 108–109. Translated by Ramin S. Khanjani.

Dear Ahmad Talebinejad,

I'm so grateful for your letter. As usual, your letter included friendly compliments and words of praise, which I'm grateful for. You also mentioned that you see me as a friend. Besides, jealousy is not your thing, and it's too late in life to make enemies. I understand and believe your words.

Eleven years ago, coming back from my first international festival at Cannes, I was welcomed by a good friend. He congratulated me and, just before we parted, asked: "How many awards did you get?" "Three," I replied. "You're in for real trouble," he said. "Now you have 3,000 enemies."

At that time his words didn't quite sink in, but as I continued to work and the number of awards grew over the years, losing friends and gaining enemies became something ordinary. Now even when friends like you write to me, they try to be very even-handed so as not to give anyone a reason to be offended. But your letter gives me an opportunity to answer some of the questions I have skirted all these years in an effort to avoid misunderstandings; and since you mentioned that you're a friend of mine, I feel obliged to give you a response.

My dear critic friend, I should thank you for sympathizing with me over the illegal distribution of *Offside;* it's great that you react to the suppression of cultural expression and, unlike many others, do not condone it. You write: "The authorities' stance towards the subject matter that you pick is well known. Therefore it would be pointless to expect them to issue screening permits for films of social criticism." I imagine that your intention is not to invite me to drink from "the fountain of forgetfulness." Or at least I hope you don't mean that, that I should fit myself into the mold of the authorities' tastes, wait and see what kind of film gets their seal of approval, and then adapt myself to their preferences; or that I should avoid sensitive subject matter altogether, but that if I do pick such subjects, I should present them in a way that pleases the officials. What then would happen to Jafar Panahi? Where's the guy who, as you mentioned yourself, broke onto the filmmaking scene with diligence and tenacity, and whom you praised as a role model for young people? Is a role model supposed to capitulate to the authorities' demands? All these years I've been encouraged to commit self-censorship, and asked to relent. But what should I have conceded? Why would I have allowed my films and thoughts to be butchered? For whose pleasure? I've said this multiple times, and now I'm repeating myself: When I'm making a film, and especially during its production, I never concern myself with censorship, sales, or whether or not the film will be liked by the authorities, viewers, local or international festivals, or friends and enemies. These must not be my concern during production, or else the film would not be mine. I consider these problems and find a solution only after the film is made.

I know this is a dangerous thing to do and could set my whole life on fire.

When I met Amir Naderi[1] in New York after so many years, we chatted about various things before he got to the point: "Jafar! When you are able to set fire to your entire life and create your life anew so that is better than before, that would be the moment when you could make your own film. Filmmakers cannot make their own films until they have achieved self-sufficiency. Don't get emotionally attached to anything in your life."

My dear filmmaker friend! To make my own films, I decided first to be honest with myself in any given situation, to have no fear of who I am, and under no circumstances to conceal my emotions. I am whatever I am—good, bad, or ugly. I try to overcome my fears of what might happen to me or my films. Hence, whenever I have felt a film must be made, I have made it without worrying myself about the opinions of parliament members and critics alike. My duty has been to artistically and historically document social situations in my country, and I have accomplished that.

Now you're saying that plenty of rumors are being told behind my back. So be it. These rumors, whether negative or positive, have no impact on the route I've already taken. These rumors are nothing but an invitation to drink from the fountain of forgetfulness. You probably remember that story from *Serpico*: There was a spring, drinking from which would make everyone mad, and there was someone who refused to drink from that spring. He was eventually forced to drink, and became like the others. Next day there was no mad person in the city, and, of course, there was no one to object.

A few days ago I was discussing the value of a single frame with my son, who's studying at film school. I told him that in my adolescence, I used my first wages to buy a camera. I pampered that camera and wouldn't take it out of the box lightly. I wouldn't allow an image to pass through my lens and be committed to film stock until I was sure of its purpose and sacredness. My friend, do you know where I learned about the sanctity of image and cinema? I learned it from the films and film critics of that time, critics who perceived every detail of cinema as a sign of the director's power and grandeur. They made cinema look so important to us! But what has now become of that sacred status?

Our story today is not much different from the digital cameras that enable thousands of images to pass through the lens and become so jumbled that the exceptional image and the golden frame get lost. But, my dear Talebinejad, I can no longer speak to my son about that sacred frame. Do you know why? Today's Iranian film journalism reminds me of crass, shallow Los Angeles-based Iranian TV channels, whose tone and style of speech have spread to the Iranian press. They focus on the trivia surrounding cinema instead of on cinema itself, and they circulate rumors about filmmakers' private lives in lieu of film criticism. What they publish might appear under different writers' names, but which of them will we remember? The generation of film critics who wrote of resistance, honesty, and seeking justice has not been forgotten, has it? In all honesty, I'm committed to nothing but my own conscience. I have made no commitment to making social problem films forever. But whatever film I make, irrespective of its form or genre, I feel an obligation to maintain the sanctity of its every frame.

My scriptwriter friend, you wrote: "You know that if you make, for instance, a film about a few female prisoners who are on a short leave from prison . . . your film will invariably court censorship." Yes, I understand this subject will run into problems. What I don't understand is why we have accepted censorship so easily and found it justifiable. I know where and under what conditions we live. My issue is with the implication that *The Circle* ought not have been made because of these conditions. More severe and sensitive topics have been made into films in a way that embraced censorship and sanction. Should I have made my film in the same spirit? Have you ever asked yourself why my films are subjected to censorship? Hasn't it been exactly because I didn't want to make films to please others, and to sweeten bitter social realities? You're saying that you like *The Circle* despite its excessively dark subject matter. Please be fair. What part of *The Circle* is exaggerated or removed from reality? Together let's go over some of the restrictions on women's rights so that you get the whole picture.

Why are we so scared of realities being shown? Isn't it because we refuse to believe that we have turned into ineffectual people who have resigned ourselves to live under any given condition? Is it I who have infused this darkness into a film that has so far been denied an official public screening? In my opinion, and echoing what you've said, a public screening of *The Circle* could have held a mirror up before a society that wants to forget its ugliness. Isn't *not* showing *The Circle* itself a proof of these bitter realities? And hasn't this situation taken a turn for the worse since *The Circle* was made? As a filmmaker, should I close my eyes to the realities of society, or consent to have eighteen minutes of my film cut, so that I may avoid your charge of making too dark a film? The very first excision of a single frame from any of my films would negate my effort of ten years. Censoring my films is no longer a personal issue. You know better than I do that in addition to perseverance, I have to inspire the young people with resistance. You are asking me to support Iranian social cinema. You are asking me to lend my support to art works that are in conflict with official regulations. I'm a filmmaker, and my films provide social critiques that, from the standpoint of the authorities, are at odds with their agenda. This is how I lend my support. No matter the cost, I will not retreat—otherwise I would have been better off investing all the effort I have put into making my own films into any other enterprise, and gained a larger profit.

My filmmaker friend, you wrote: "Some people believe that despite your vocal protests against the state for banning your last few movies, you're not as discontented as you'd have us believe, because you are able to exploit your notoriety by marketing your films abroad." "Some people believe," that is how you put it; but who and where are these people you refer to? If you know them, tell me from where their beliefs spring. Is it flowing from some underlying information or knowledge, or is it some unfounded assertion they use as cover? Are you telling me what I should do, about people who don't have the slightest knowledge of marketing Iranian films abroad, and who, in order to make up for their ignorance, and driven by their conspiracy theories, make the most spurious and irrelevant assumptions?

The sales and marketing of Iranian films routinely start with their premieres on the international festival circuit. If a film shows promise for international distribution, eighty percent of its international sales deals will be made during that very first festival. Because of the scheduling, with which you're very familiar, Iranian films are usually entered into the festivals at the last minute, before any decision has been made to screen them in Iran and before there has been any opportunity to promote them. So how can a film's ban affect its international sales? Even if the film's ban is announced right after the festival, it cannot give the filmmaker any extra benefit, because sales contracts have already been signed.

Take *Offside* as an example. It was shown at the Berlinale after screening in Iran at Fajr Film Festival. I insisted on having the screening permit for *Offside* issued before my trip to Berlin, so that I could make an official announcement during the press conference that it would be screened before the World Cup. The authorities in the Ministry of Culture and Islamic Guidance promised to inform me about the permit on Wednesday. I had to leave for Berlin, so I asked my wife to wait for their call on Wednesday and immediately inform me of their decision. No news came on Wednesday, so at the press conference, unfortunately, I could only express my hope that the screening permit for *Offside* would be issued quickly. I've been waiting for a call ever since, and *Offside* still hasn't been either banned or granted a screening permit. Could publicizing this situation have any impact on the sales of *Offside?*

You added: "A friend has seen with his own eyes the poster for *Crimson Gold* somewhere overseas, at the top of which it was written that the film doesn't have a permit for screening in Iran." He's seen that correctly and has told you the truth. Maybe two out of thirty distributors have pulled this publicity stunt. So what? Have they lied? Take as an instance *Valley of the Wolves: Iraq,* which is now in the-aters in Tehran; hasn't its ban in the States been used in its press and advertise-ments? Even our state TV channel, airing foreign films, proudly boasts when any of them have been banned. Now, on the other side of the globe, two distributors opted for the same gimmick; what has it to do with me? I might have a bit of say over some international posters of my film, and the distributor might respect my request and make some changes to them, but it's not in my power to supervise the design of all the posters all over the world, and neither is it my responsibility. It's part of the distributor's duties.

You probably know that film posters mention any festival achievements or any comparisons that have been made to masterpieces of cinema, in order to attract an audience. Why, then, is your friend so selective, and of all these items—of which you can see plenty of examples on posters in the showcases at the museum of cinema—why does he concentrate on my distributor's promotion of my film's ban? Why hasn't your friend noticed that the international posters of *Crimson Gold* draw comparisons to Martin Scorsese's *Taxi Driver,* Jim Jarmusch's *Ghost Dog,* and Al Pacino's acting in *Dog Day Afternoon?* Don't these friends of yours always claim that mainstream audiences don't come to watch our films, and that they are seen only by a small group of highbrow, intellectual spectators? What matters more to these highbrow spectators, the 4- and 5-star ratings by renowned critics or the film's ban?

And doesn't your friend belong to the same group that uses any pretext to bash these films? I remember when we were shooting the first shot of *The Mir-ror*—which, contrary to your opinion, I view as an important film—at Jomhoori intersection, a critic friend who happened to be passing by, and who loathed *The White Balloon,* half-jokingly remarked: "Now you're making films without making any noise. It doesn't matter. I've already done its review. I'll be your killjoy." Dear Talebinejad, both of us know that this killjoy of a film critic is one of the 3,000 enemies my esteemed friend was referring to.

You'd better know that, according to its American distributor, not show-ing *Crimson Gold* cost Iranian cinema its chance of being in competition for an

Academy Award. You very well know how even being an Academy Award nominee can boost a film's box office. Do you remember the letter from the distributor of *Crimson Gold* to the Deputy Minister for Cinematic Affairs, and the request it contained? Did the letter ask for the film to be banned in order to boost sales, or was it asking for a public screening of *Crimson Gold* in Iran, lest it lose its eligibility for Oscar nomination? Never mind. Nowadays forgetfulness reigns supreme.

My dear Talebinejad, you wrote: "Some believe there's a contradiction between the lifestyles of people like you—who have a reputation for being socially sensitive and commiserating with the underprivileged—and what their works show. If it can be established that "poverty" has been the "merchandise" to make more money, and if there is a huge gap between an artist's lifestyle and what's pictured in their films, at least some doubts can be raised about the artist's honesty." Is poverty the central issue in my films? Even if that is true to a degree in *The White Balloon,* what could be said of *The Mirror*? Is its main theme poverty or is it about a schizoid society? Which one is the central theme of *The Circle*, poverty or lack of security and mobility? Does *Crimson Gold* speak about poverty, or does it speak about tremendous class divisions? What does *Offside* deal with, poverty or existing legal restrictions? Let's imagine that I *have* made my films about poverty—and if this were the case, I'd see nothing wrong with it; isn't it true that I've experienced poverty more than anything else in thirty-seven out of forty-seven years of my life? You believe that an artist ought to primarily express their own experiences. How could you imagine that these last ten years have effaced from my memory that experience of living in poverty? Those years formed the foundation of my life, and I cannot forget my roots. Indeed, I'm still struggling with the ramifications of my early experiences and trying to fill the seemingly never-ending financial holes. I still belong to the same class as before, so it wouldn't be too much of a reach for me to talk about it. But is talking about humanity, deprivations, and restrictions the prerogative of a particular class? Please don't take my analogy seriously, but was Victor Hugo, who penned *Les Miserables*, a poor man? Were Rossellini, De Sica, and in particular Visconti, who founded Neorealism, gripped by poverty? I'm sure there must be a misunderstanding here. Let's not instruct our friends on the censorship board to compare a director's chosen genre with his bank account.

My friend of fifteen years, you've asked me why I don't age. I must say that the famous wish "May you reach an old age"[2] doesn't work for most of my family members, because the majority of them *don't* reach an advanced age, and depart this life in middle age. My dad passed away at the age of fifty-three, my uncle expired at about the same age, and my sister, who was the eldest sibling, died a few days ago from a cerebral stroke. I am forty-seven now, and a while ago I told the Deputy Minister for Cinematic Affairs about this history of death in our family. I told him that I've only a few years left. These remaining years are not worth turning my back on my beliefs, because I've learned from Ingmar Bergman that any film that I make and any shot that I shoot might be my last. So I have to put all of myself into it, as if there were little precious time to work with. Amir Naderi spoke similarly: "Make your films in such a way that if you have a stroke on the set and die, your last shot turns out the best shot of your life."

See what a nice solution I've found for my short life? As a matter of fact, I use this family history as an excuse, because it encourages me to not make a bad film and gives me the courage not to capitulate to censorship and to make no concessions to others. Thinking this way makes me feel young, because I feel no need to be conservative or expedient. Not only does this way of thinking do me no harm, it probably helps me to live a longer life, for each day of which I'll be thankful to God. But if I leave this world sooner than I'd like, at the moment of death I'll have no regrets and feel no personal shame about the films that I made. Maybe thinking this way is the very essence of self-sufficiency? By the way, Ahmad, did anyone realize why Amir Naderi left the country?

Notes

1. Iranian-born filmmaker who immigrated to the United States in the 1990s. He is best known for *The Runner* (1984), a prototype of Iran's post-revolution art cinema (i.e., neorealist, starring a child).
2. An expression in Farsi used for wishing someone a long life.

Jafar Panahi Interview (Parts One and Two)

Peter Keough / 2009

From *Boston Phoenix,* September 25/28, 2009. Reprinted by permission from the author.

A couple of days ago, as reported in the *New York Times,* Mahmoud Ahmadinejad proclaimed to the UN that the Iranian "people entrusted me once more with a large majority" in a ballot he described as "glorious and fully democratic." Wordlessly and far more eloquently earlier this month the great Iranian filmmaker Jafar Panahi challenged that claim when he and the other members of the jury for the Montreal Film Festival took the stage wearing green scarves—green being the color of those opposing Ahmadinejad's regime.

Panahi, who has been barred from filmmaking and whose last three movies (*The Circle* [2000], *Crimson Gold* [2003], and *Offside* [2006]) have been banned in his native land, therefore must employ other means to express himself—such as the following interview.

Peter Keough: Tell me about the green scarves.
Jafar Panahi: It was my own idea. I bought the scarves in Tehran and brought them here. I asked the jury if they would wear them and fortunately they accepted.

PK: And earlier as you walked on the red carpet to the opening ceremony you greeted a number of demonstrators. Was this spontaneous?
JP: It was spontaneous, though I wanted it to happen. When I saw those people with painted faces, it reminded me of the young people In Tehran. These green scarves and green faces don't stand for any person or party specifically but the color is a sign for the future, for hope for the future. In a country with very little water like Iran the color green is a symbol of hope for the future and for civilization. It's a symbol of resistance to the government and freedom. The basic rights of the people. I am a part of this society and I have had all these sorts of problems. For four years I haven't had the right to make a movie. I felt that since they no longer let me make movies, and since it had been almost a year and a half since I

have gone to a festival, I felt that now was a good time to go to one and express my feelings. And even though filmmakers can't make movies, now we have thousands of amateur filmmakers in the streets of Tehran who can make movies that transfigure reality with their cell phones and put it online. In Iran all the media are controlled by the government, so there isn't any other place. We don't have privately owned TV. All the cinemas and everything are under the control of the government. All the newspapers and journals. There are some that are semi-independent, but if anything happens they would close them all. Most of the journalists are in prison. In such a situation, filmmakers should be with the people.

PK: Are you worried about returning to Iran after voicing your opinion so openly here?

JP: When I'm in Iran I have the same attitude. A week before I came here I was arrested with my family and some documentary people just because we went to the cemetery for Neda.[1] This oppression exists everywhere in the country. Whether you leave or come back, it's the same for everyone in the country.

PK: What happened when you were arrested?

JP: I was arrested at eleven o'clock. I knew I should somehow communicate to people in the outside cinema world that I was arrested. I came up with a clever way to do so. And when I did so the word went out to everybody in the cinema world what had happened to me. Some of those people came to where I was arrested and they put on pressure and somehow they were obligated to let me go. At around half past seven they released me. But during these eight hours there was very good media coverage about what had happened. It shows the power of the cinema. They know they cannot easily face the people of cinema with impunity. The government media announced that Panahi was arrested "mistakenly." They know how to avoid telling the truth.

PK: Was this international pressure or just from Iranian filmmakers?

JP: From all over the world. I heard that some very famous filmmakers were planning to do something very serious if I was detained any longer.

PK: Because you are a filmmaker are you immune from the kind of repression suffered by the ordinary Iranian?

JP: The country is so closed to the outside world that they can do anything they want with the people. They will reach a point where it's very difficult for them to back down and at that point this kind of government can only think about a huge massacre. We know that's what's going to happen but we don't know when.

PK: So you aren't very optimistic.

JP: The people who are in power don't want to lose it. They have engaged in the worst possible behavior in the prisons in Iran. If what they have done to these prisoners had not been communicated to the outside, for sure they would have denied the abuses and shooting, but with the tiny cell phones this has been transmitted to the outside and other evidence has been documented.

PK: One of the recurrent symbols in your films is the circle. Do you find it ironic that the history of Iran has been circular, with the revolutionaries of thirty years ago now repressing a revolution themselves?

JP: Exactly. But now it's more difficult compared to thirty years ago. Because now it's an ideological government. A dictatorial government is better than an ideological government. Because that ideological government has its own dictatorship and a religious ideology that connects itself to God so they can apply their dictatorship even more tyrannically.

PK: So if there's change it will be much bloodier than the overthrow of the Shah?

JP: It's not predictable. In the summer before the revolution, if you had asked someone if there might be a revolution, a very optimistic person would say maybe in a century. Yet six months later it happened. My optimistic opinion is that the people in Iran are practicing democracy on the street. I was with those people on the street. There were almost two million of them and I walked with them for an hour. Not one person said anything. There was total silence. You can't find this anywhere in the world.

But although they want to be united, the government is trying to turn the people against one another. I hope this experience of tolerating each other will continue to be practiced and we will be able to keep our country unified. But I'm afraid if they don't succeed at that they will destroy the country because we have many different nations in Iran. As has been seen in the similar experiences of the USSR, in the former Yugoslavia, and in Afghanistan and Iraq, huge problems can arise.

Our main goal is to be unified and tolerate each other and not just to eliminate the people in power. That's the only way we can reach our goal. So that green color is a symbol of that hope. It's not in support of Mousavi[2] or any other individual. We are demonstrating for that future, that everyone might be unified under this color. Our goal is not supporting any particular person or government. We have a higher responsibility. Any time I have a bad feeling about what's happening, like about that closed circle that is in the movie *The Circle*, I think of another movie I made, *Offside*, where there is shown a small hope of breaking free.

[Part Two follows]

Here are two kinds of political demonstrations. First, the Iranian Revolutionary Guards test-firing a ballistic missile with a range sufficient to hit Israel, Moscow, parts of Europe and US military targets as a way to break the ice for an upcoming meeting in Geneva on Thursday with U.N. Security council members to discuss its nuclear program.

Second, as reported in the IFC website, Iranian filmmakers Hana and Samira Makhmalbaf, following the lead of Jafar Panahi earlier this month in Montreal, peacefully demonstrated last Thursday at the San Sebastian Film Festival against the Ahmadinejad regime with a hundred other protesters carrying green flags and calling for peace and democracy.

Neither has gone unnoticed. The latter, according to IFC, has stirred Ahmadinejad's art advisor Javad Shamaqdari to threaten " . . . a boycott of festivals by 'Iranian artists' if protests continued. 'The enemy, which has been disappointed concerning their plans for a velvet coup and a soft war in Iran, tries to keep up the fever of their subversive activities at foreign art and cinematic events,' he announced. 'The Venice film festival was a vulgar display revealing the enemy's plan.'"

Vulgar, I suppose, when compared to firing a missile and escalating tensions that could lead to a horrendous regional if not worldwide conflict. Be that as it may, a test of Shamaqdari's boycott threat might take place when Panahi attends the Mumbai Film Festival as president of its jury. The festival starts October 29.

Meanwhile, here's the second half of my interview with Panahi at Montreal, which picks up after his mentioning of his films *The Circle* and *Offside*. [Note that the interview is made through an interpreter.]

PK: But both those films were banned in Iran. Can we still expect Iran to continue to be the great national cinema it has been?

JP: The production in the cinema industry in Iran will not stop. There are more of the cheap government movies than ever. But a year ago in an interview I had predicted that there will be an underground cinema in Iran. We saw one such film at the Cannes Festival by Bahman Ghobadi,[3] which will also be showing at San Sebastian. There are many other movies that are produced in this way. In a country like ours, if they stop filmmakers in one way they will find another way.

PK: What about your own filmmaking?

JP: I have a film I want to make about the last day of the Iran-Iraq War. The story is ready. I want to make it. I hope I can do it in Iran. If not, then somewhere else, a place that is like Iran geographically. But I prefer to do it in Iran. Because I have always preferred that Iranian filmmakers should not go outside the country. Some have been obligated to leave the country. But I think we should stay here and use the Iranian setting to make movies. Maybe one day I'll leave the country to make a movie but I'll come back again. However, now my goal is to make movies in Iran. I have a lot of stories already prepared. If they let me do so after I come back, I can start my work.

PK: Do you think your outspokenness here and, presumably next month when you serve as the president of the jury at Mumbai, will cause problems for you when you try to make your next film?

JP: There are problems always. But I never censor myself and I never let them censor my films. I will never let anyone remove one frame. I have always said I would never let anyone change one frame. That's my belief. If I censor myself in that way the movies won't be mine. When I went to the US and they wanted to fingerprint me I did not let them. If I didn't accept that then there, then I won't accept any violations of my rights anywhere.

PK: Can you describe that experience and compare it to your arrest in Iran?

JP: It's not comparable. The US has its own laws. If I'm going there as a tourist I should obey its laws. But I was invited there as an artist. It was an insult to myself and my profession. But I am willing to suffer more in my country than anywhere else because there I want to change the situation. And create something ideal. But the laws of another country are their own. I can be opposed to them. But my actions in my country are not just a protest but also a discussion to try to build something. If you can't build something, then you suffer more.

PK: Did you have any difficulties attending this festival after you were arrested?

JP: No, I had no problem. I don't need their permission.

PK: There are some Iranian movies in this festival, including a short by your son. Can you comment on these?

JP: I've not watched the others as yet. I've seen my son's film and I liked it. What happened was that they were collecting the satellite dishes in his neighborhood. My son is a student at a university in Tehran. He took his camera and he started to make a documentary about this.

PK: Is it like those films you described before taken by people covertly with cell phones?

JP: Even in your own home you can make a movie.

PK: In the West people tend to dismiss film as just entertainment. Do you believe that film has an important political role?

JP: Yes. Since everything is under the control of the government here, if there is a movie that they don't have control over and which shows the reality of the people, the people will believe in it. Maybe in your country a filmmaker doesn't have the problems we have in our country. Maybe in your country the problem is commercial and financial. So the situations aren't comparable. In my country it isn't a question of money; it's a question of how you dress, what you eat, what you can do. Everything is controlled in Iran. When you're in Iran you're used to that so when there's just a little deviation the government reacts strongly to stop it but people will look for it to see it. They'll get it from satellite dishes and pirated DVDs. When *Offside* was banned, two days later the whole country had copies of the DVD. So the government has intensified curiosity about those films they have banned. It reminds me of some lines of dialogue from *The White Balloon*. The little girl wants to go see something but her parents wouldn't let her. When the grandmother asks her why she wants to go anyway, she says, "I wanted to see what they didn't want me to see."

PK: Unlike the Hollywood studios, then, you don't disapprove of having your work pirated?

JP: I want my movies to be seen. That's my hope. If my films are broadcast everywhere else in the world they should also be seen in my own country. Actually, the government thinks I'm behind the pirating. That's because in the case of *Offside* I asked the government to let me release the film before the World Cup. They didn't let me, but twenty days before the World Cup a pirated copy was distributed anyway. They thought this was my plan. I said, I think this is your plan to destroy me financially.

PK: Andrzej Wajda has a film[4] in this festival. It made me wonder if there might be a *Man of Iron*-kind of film made about the current crisis in Iran. What's your thought on this?

JP: It's completely unpredictable. There's a huge potential for anything. It could end up a bloody massacre. If it continues in this way there will be disaster for both sides.

PK: Can people outside Iran do anything to help the situation?

JP: Absolutely not. Everyone in Iran would be unified against any country that wants to do anything to Iran. With any such action freedom and democracy in Iran will die. There will be an even stronger dictatorship in our country if any country interferes.

PK: What film did you see that inspired you to become a filmmaker yourself?

JP: It was a long time ago. One film had a huge influence on me. It was *Bicycle Thieves* by Vittorio De Sica. At the beginning of the film Ricci has his bicycle stolen. In the end he tries to steal a bicycle himself. It was such a big influence on me that I wanted to make *The Circle* in another way. A new story on the same theme.

PK: Good luck with the green scarves.

JP: I hope it gets some results. In Tehran I was informed that there was a wonderful reaction. A newspaper in Tehran that's quite independent put the photo on the front page. Given the circumstances, that's really something.

Notes

1. A young woman shot during an anti-Ahmadinejad demonstration who has become a symbol of the movement.
2. Mir-Hossein Mousavi is the opposition candidate defeated by Ahmadinejad in the disputed election.
3. The 2009 film *No One Knows About the Persian Cats* (*Kasi az gorbehaye Irani khabar nadareh*).
4. The 2009 film *Sweet Rush* (*Tatarak*).

Jafar Panahi's Video Statement on ARTE

Jafar Panahi / 2010

From *ARTE* (excerpted and rebroadcast on *BBC Persian*), May 27, 2010. http://www.bbc.com/persian/arts/2010/06/100603_u03-aa-panahi. Translated by Iante Roach.

Editor's preface: Two days after Jafar Panahi was released on bail from Evin Prison in Tehran (May 25), he gave this video statement in his own home. First broadcast on ARTE, the French-German TV station, the video installment was later excerpted and shown on BBC Persian from London.

I'm sitting in the house where they came to arrest me for the crime of making films.

Whether filmmaking is a crime is another matter. But it seems that the real problem is the fear of me making films. This fear never leaves them, not even when I'm in prison. I remember one day, actually one night, they came into my cell and took me and my cellmates out and started searching us frantically. It took a long time, about an hour, and I did not know why this was happening. The following morning I was summoned to an interrogation. The first thing the interrogator said was: "What is its name?"

"What are you talking about?"

"The name of your film," he said.

"Well, you did not let me finish my film, it's an unfinished work. When I make a film, I choose an initial title, but it can change; I understand new things about the film through making it."

"No, I'm not talking about the film you were making at home, I mean the film you have been making here."

"Where?" I asked.

"Inside your cell."

"How is it possible to make a film inside a cell?"

He truly believed that I was making a film inside my cell, that smugglers had brought me a camera or something of the sort! Within this high-security prison—you couldn't even imagine how to smuggle anything into it. Yet he believed that I was making a film there, and the whole interrogation continued in this vein. I kept denying it until they threatened to put my whole family into the same prison. When I realized that their paranoia was creating security problems for my family, I announced I would begin a hunger strike. It turned out that when one of my cell-mates spoke to his family on the phone and they asked him, among other things, how I was doing, he would say that I was well, that I behaved in such and such a way, and that I was making a film about my life! It appears that my cellmate's phone was tapped. So they really imagined that I had brought a camera into the cell and was making a film inside the prison. All these interactions and interrogations had to do with their imaginings and fear that I was making a film.

But no matter what, I cannot not work, not think or dream, about making films. You have to keep going in some way, and for me life is making films. I might be obliged to make films only in my dreams or inside my mind. Whatever happens, will happen.

Jafar Panahi's Defense

Jafar Panahi / 2010

Printed with permission of the author. Translated by Iante Roach. This version is slightly abridged.

Editor's preface: In the wake of Iran's "stolen election" of 2009, many analysts and nations, including the United States, doubted the validity of the election. Opposition candidate Mir-Hossein Mousavi has claimed that as many as fourteen million unused ballots went missing. In response, the Green Movement was born. Millions of Iranians took to the streets with slogans such as "Where is my vote?" They wore green scarves and wristbands in protest, many demanding that President Mahmoud Ahmadinejad step down. As many were imprisoned in the days and weeks following the election. Panahi, a vocal supporter of Mousavi and the Green Movement, began making a film on the events surrounding the election and was himself arrested, this time in his own home. On the evening of March 1, 2010, officers from the Ministry of Intelligence took him and up to seventeen other people, including fellow Iranian filmmaker Mohammad Rasoulof, film crew, and family, to Evin Prison. Later that year, on December 20, 2010, before Branch 26 of the Islamic Revolutionary Tribunal, Panahi was found guilty of collusion, assembly, and making propaganda against the Islamic Republic. The month before, he read this prepared statement to the same court, in hopes of persuading them towards lenience.

Esteemed Tribunal President, I would like to present my own defense in two parts:

First Part: What They Say

Over the last few days I again watched films that I love and have watched many times (though of course I did not have access to many films that are important in the history of cinema). On the night of March 1, 2010, while Mr. Mohammad Rasoulof[1] and I were shooting my latest film, a work in the style of social and art cinema, the security forces, who introduced themselves as officials from the Ministry of Intelligence arrested us and our colleagues without showing us an arrest warrant. They also took away the films from my personal collection and never gave them back to me. The only time I ever heard anything about these films was when the interrogator in charge of my case asked me, "What are these obscene films that were in your possession?"

I learned filmmaking from those same movie classics that my interrogator called obscene. I honestly do not know how anyone could call them obscene, just as I do not understand how anyone could define the charges that you are trying me for, as crimes. Is this not a clear case of retribution before crime? You are bringing me to court for making a new film, but when I was arrested on set we had not yet even filmed thirty percent of the film's scenes. You have certainly heard the saying that if you pronounce only the first half of the declaration "There is no God but God"[2] in order to testify to the oneness of God, it is considered an act of atheism. How is it possible to accuse someone of making a film when referring only to a third of its scenes, well before it can even have been edited and undergone sound mixing, and way before the other post-production stages are completed? Let me shoot the rest of the film, edit it, do the sound mixing, finish all the post-production, and then you may judge it. It is a socially conscious film, based on the efforts of a family to reclaim hope and reunite again.

I really cannot find a way to understand your sense of "obscenity" or the accusations leveled against me. If I am right, you are bringing not only us to court, you are bringing to court all the art cinema and socially minded cinema of Iran—a cinema in which neither entirely positive nor entirely negative human beings exist, a cinema that does not serve the interests of money or power, a cinema that does not believe in siding with a character or villainizing him, but that examines society honestly from the viewpoint of the filmmaker, a cinema that is inspired by acute social problems and that therefore deals first and foremost with humanity.

In the accusations against us, it has been said that we wanted to encourage protest and sedition with our new film. During all these years of filmmaking I have always said, and say again now, that I am a socially engaged filmmaker, not a political filmmaker. My chief concerns are social, and this is why my films are humanist rather than political. I believe that political cinema lacks artistic value. Political cinema is partisan, propagandistic, and ideological. Political cinema gives orders to its spectators, what to do and what not to do. Political cinema administers partisan pills to the audience, insulting their intelligence.

I have chosen to make films that are engaged socially rather than politically. Even back on the day I graduated from university, I swore to practice and protect this sort of cinema, just like doctors who swear the Hippocratic Oath. I still adhere to my oath. This has made for many complications up to the present day, and has resulted in the detention of filmmakers like myself. But there is no precedent in Iranian cinema of a filmmaker being arrested and sent to prison for the "crime" of making a film. And likewise it has never happened before that the family of a filmmaker would be attacked in their home and be subject to death threats and intimidation while he was in prison. This is a shift in the history of Iranian cinema, and it will be spoken about forever.

I was accused of attending demonstrations. In socially minded cinema, filmmakers are observers. We observe events in our society and document our culture as it changes. But filmmakers observe through our cameras, and no Iranian filmmakers are allowed to use their cameras. Filmmakers observe their surroundings so that maybe one day they will be inspired to create a work of art. I was an observer, and it was my right to see. Nobody has the right to force an artist not to see. Why is it necessary to deprive an artist of this right and bring him into court for an imaginary crime?

It has been said that we were making the film without a permit. First of all, we must say that there exists no law approved by Parliament and communicated to the Ministry of Culture and Islamic Guidance in this regard. There exist only internal regulations that are susceptible to the whims of the director of the film division.

It has been said that we did not give a script to the actors of the film. Usually cinema is divided into two categories: commercial, studio cinema and art cinema. Commercial cinema is made with professional actors. They know their profession very well. They can construct their characters by reading the script with the guidance of the director. But in art cinema, and especially in my kind of social realist cinema, most of the actors are nonprofessional. In these films, directors do not see the need to give them a script, because doing so affects their performance negatively. If you are going to bring us to court for this crime, you are also bringing to court many great filmmakers who work in this way. This is a filmmaking methodology that has not been prohibited judicially or legally. These particular accusations in my case really seem like a joke.

I have been accused of signing a declaration. I did sign a declaration by thirty-seven Iranian filmmakers. At a time when many groups throughout all levels of society were issuing public declarations in response to events in Iran, thirty-seven of Iran's most acclaimed filmmakers declared their concern for the future of this country. I was one of them. Unfortunately, instead of paying attention to the concerns raised by artists who love their country, this court singled out certain parts of the statement and turned them into criminal evidence. Is it a crime to love one's country and express concern over its direction? Did these thirty-seven filmmakers not have the right to express their opinion on the situation in Iran? And must these thirty-seven individuals be tried? These thirty-seven filmmakers are the same people who express their reaction to every kind of injustice anywhere in the world, by writing declarations. How can they now be expected to be indifferent to the destiny of their country?

I would like to remind you that in a country where anyone can easily be accused of being a traitor or a spy, so far no filmmaker has been accused of such a crime.

It has been said that I was responsible for organizing demonstrations abroad, during the opening night of the Montreal Film Festival in Canada. Every accusation must eventually be backed up by some truth, however. I was the President of the Jury in Montreal and only arrived there a few hours before the ceremony. How could I have done all this organizing in so little time and without knowing anyone there? Have we really forgotten that, at that same time, our fellow compatriots abroad were assembling to demonstrate at all sorts of ceremonies, wherever they were? Even at sporting events! So now, must athletes, including the soccer players who were wearing green wristbands, or the coach of the national team, also be accused of organizing their audience in protest?

It has been said that I gave interviews to the Persian-language press abroad. Is there a law that forbids us to give interviews? Yet this is the only matter for which, in September of last year, I received a serious warning from the Ministry of Interior.

Second Part: What I Say

History shows that artists analyze the society around them. Through their lenses and from their vantage points, they observe the events taking place around them. They analyze what they see and incorporate their observations into artworks that are meant to be seen, known and judged by society—and that may even help politicians see the way ahead. Should artists be criminalized for the inner workings of their minds? Is not my arrest—and those of my colleagues and family—for the concocted crime of making a film without a permit—a sign to all Iranians who work in the arts that whoever is independent and not ready to accept artistic prostitution must go to prison?

Repressing beliefs the moment they are conceived and "sterilizing" artists who care for their society can only have one result: to dry up of the roots of free thought and to render the tree of creative art fruitless. I think that arresting me and my colleagues while we were shooting an unfinished film is an attack perpetrated by those in power on all Iranian filmmakers, artists, and cultural figures. It is a show of power that says that whoever is not on our side and does not think like us is to be condemned.

Iranian cinema over the last thirty years has been the pride of Iran and a beacon of Iranian art. Having made all my films in this country that I call home, I am proud to have contributed to this legacy. Yet I am just a filmmaker. In most respects I am removed from politics and power struggles. By arresting me and bringing me to court, however, you have politicized me and my cinema. For it is not only I who am on trial. All art and artists of this country stand trial today. As much as history does forget some facts, rest assured that it will never forget how artists are treated.

Whatever verdict you reach will be a verdict on Iranian society, whose people have been the intended audience of my films. However you sentence me, so too will you sentence the people of this country.

In the future, this day will not be remembered as the day of Jafar Panahi's trial, but rather as the day Iranian art and cinema went on trial.

Does anyone remember that, nine years ago when he was invited to a film festival in America, Jafar Panahi declared that he would not go if he had to give his fingerprints at the border? And indeed he did not go.

Sometime later he accepted invitations to attend film festivals in Argentina and Uruguay. En route, while he was changing planes at a New York airport, customs officials summoned him for the humiliating procedure of being fingerprinted because of anti-terrorism laws targeting Iranian citizens. Jafar Panahi refused to obey, enduring sixteen hours of interrogation and leaving the following day to return to his country.

His response was to protest this sort of racial and regional profiling, which subjects Iranians and many others to second-class humiliation. This resulted in widespread support from international organizations and figures the world over. Because, you see, independent artists and groups oppose injustice all over the world without prejudice. They are not dependent on any power or party. They declare their opinions in any place and time, far removed from the machinations of politics. Little did Jafar Panahi know that one day he would be arrested in his own country—and go to Evin Prison handcuffed—for raising the very same concerns about justice and oppression, only in a different place and time.

Does anyone in this tribunal remember that Jafar Panahi has not been able to make films in this country for five years, that two years ago he was denied a permit to make his film *Return* about the Iran-Iraq War, and that he was unable to release and screen his films in theaters, whether or not they had been granted permits?

Does anyone in this tribunal remember last September, when Jafar Panahi, after his passport had been seized at the airport and he was barred from leaving Iran, declared in a joint statement with two other filmmakers, also barred from leaving the country, "We are filmmakers. We could have chosen to have a different passport during all our years of artistic and cultural activity. But we chose to remain Iranian"? At the time, Jafar Panahi did not know that remaining in his country would come hand in hand with being arrested and placed in solitary confinement.

Does anyone in this court remember that the booth that contains Jafar Panahi's awards and prizes at the Museum of Cinema is much bigger than his solitary
confinement cell?

Whether we remember these matters or not, I, Jafar Panahi, declare once more
that I am Iranian and will always remain so, even if that means imprisonment. I
love my country and I have paid dearly for it. If it is necessary, I shall do so again.
And since, as my films testify, I believe that mutual understanding, respect, and
tolerance are principles of civilization, I would like to stress that I do not bear any
ill will toward Iran or even toward my interrogators. For we are all accountable to
the next generation, to whom we must hand this country over as gracefully and
peacefully as possible.

History is patient. Every period passes sooner or later. But I am worried and
I plead with you to explore your own consciences. I am worried about divisions
born of hate that threaten to tear this country apart at the seams. I wanted, and
still want, peace, tolerance, and mutual respect to be the basis of our social and
human relations. I want future generations to learn humanity, freedom, equality,
and fraternity from us. It is our duty to respect each other's beliefs and root out
all malice; to steer clear of tendencies that encourage any sort of social, ethnic, or
national chauvinism. If we do not do so, our Iran will become increasingly vulner-
able to chaos and insecurity—one need not look any further than our neighbor-
ing countries to see vivid examples of this. We can avoid a similar fate only if we
replace our fears and grudges with love and tolerance. This is the path that will
guarantee the preservation and honor of Iran.

"Love's path is a path whereof the shore is none . . ."[3]

Thank you,
Jafar Panahi, Iranian filmmaker

Notes

1. Another prominent Iranian filmmaker.
2. This is the beginning of the *Shahada,* "the testimony," in Arabic *lā ʾilāha ʾillā llāh.* In Arabic as
   in English, if you stop after the first phrase, you have literally said, "There is no God."
3. Quotation from Ghazal number 72 by Shams-al-Din Mohammad Hafez of Shiraz (ca. 1315
   –1390), generally considered Iran's greatest lyric poet.

An Open Letter to the Berlin Film Festival

Jafar Panahi / 2011

Read by Isabella Rossellini at the 61st Berlin International Film Festival, February 10, 2011.

The world of a filmmaker is marked by the interplay between reality and dreams. The filmmaker uses reality as his inspiration, paints it with the color of his imagination, and creates a film that is a projection of his hopes and dreams.

The reality is that I have been kept from making films for the past five years and am now officially sentenced to be deprived of this right for another twenty years. But I know I will keep on turning my dreams into films in my imagination. I admit as a socially conscious filmmaker that I won't be able to portray the daily problems and concerns of my people, but I won't deny myself from dreaming that after twenty years, all the problems will be gone and I'll be making films about the peace and prosperity in my country when I get a chance to do so again.

The reality is that they have deprived me of thinking and writing for twenty years, but they cannot keep me from dreaming that in twenty years, inquisition and intimidation will be replaced by freedom and free thinking.

They have deprived me of seeing the world for twenty years. I hope that when I am free, I will be able to travel in a world without any geographic, ethnic, or ideological barriers, where people live together freely and peacefully regardless of their beliefs and convictions.

They have condemned me to twenty years of silence. Yet in my dreams, I scream for a time when we can tolerate each other, respect each other's opinions, and live for each other.

Ultimately, the reality of my verdict is that I must spend six years in jail. I'll live for the next six years hoping that my dreams will become reality. My wish is that my fellow filmmakers in every corner of the world will create such great films that by the time I leave prison I will be inspired to continue to live in the world they have dreamed of in their films.

So from now on, and for the next twenty years, I'm forced to be silent. I'm forced not to be able to see, I'm forced not to be able to think, I'm forced not to be able to make films.

I submit to the reality of this captivity and my captors. I will look for the manifestation of my dreams in your films, hoping to find in them what I am deprived of.

Iranian Director Flouts Ban on Filmmaking

Tobias Grey / 2014

From *The Wall Street Journal,* June 26, 2014. Reprinted with permission of the *Wall Street Journal,* Copyright © 2014 Dow Jones & Company, Inc. All Rights Reserved Worldwide. License number [from above]

In Jafar Panahi's new movie, a writer in Iran smuggles his pet dog into his home inside a tote bag. The film, *Closed Curtain*, addresses Iranian lawmakers' recent ban on dog-walking in public, part of an effort to curb perceived Western influences including keeping pets. For two decades, Mr. Panahi has captured such vagaries of life in his native country.

Closed Curtain, which won the best screenplay award at the Berlin Film Festival in 2013, opens at New York City's Film Forum on July 9. It is Mr. Panahi's second film since December 2010, when Iran's Islamic Revolutionary Court banned him from making movies for twenty years.

The fifty-three-year-old director has flouted the prohibition and continued to expand a body of work that has earned him critical acclaim around the world—and scrutiny at home. He first piqued the ire of Iranian authorities with *The Circle* (2000), which assailed the treatment of women under the country's Islamist regime. Six years later, in *Offside*, he mocked a law prohibiting Iranian women from attending professional soccer games.

As jury president of the 2009 Montreal World Film Festival, Mr. Panahi persuaded fellow jury members to wear green scarves to support Iran's pro-democratic Green Movement.

More than three years ago, Mr. Panahi was accused of spreading propaganda and undermining national security. He was found guilty and sentenced to six years in prison—time he hasn't yet served—and forbidden from traveling abroad or giving interviews.

Mr. Panahi's previous project, the documentary *This Is Not a Film* (2011), was shot almost entirely in his Tehran apartment. *Closed Curtain*, which blends fiction and autobiography, was shot exclusively in his beach house beside the Caspian

Sea. While the director is free to move throughout Iran, he isn't allowed to make movies.

Friends say Mr. Panahi chafes at the government-imposed strictures and oversight. They say that led the director to disregard the moratorium on media contact and speak with *The Wall Street Journal*.

In a recent telephone conversation—a rare interview since the sentencing—Mr. Panahi explained how the prohibitions have affected his work.

Jamsheed Akrami, a New York-based Iranian documentary maker who has known the director for twenty years, interpreted for Mr. Panahi, who spoke in Farsi during the call. Mr. Akrami, who lives in New York, then interpreted Mr. Panahi's answers into English. It isn't clear if the authorities in Tehran are aware of the conversation. Mr. Panahi's answers, edited from the interview:

Tobias Grey: In your latest film *Closed Curtain*, a neighbor visits the character whom you play and a conversation ensues. This neighbor says, "There's more to life than work, there are other things too." To which your character replies "Yes, but those things are foreign to me." Is this coming from your personal experience?

Jafar Panahi: Everybody looks at the world from his own point of view, so the neighbor in that scene is reflecting his own perspective on life and the kind of things that he's interested in. For a filmmaker, life without making movies has no meaning. His life would be reduced to a vegetative state if he's not allowed to do the kind of thing that gives it some sense.

TG: How did you feel to be banned from making movies for twenty years?

JP: Well, my immediate reaction was not to understand it. I could not understand what not making movies for twenty years would basically mean. I was thinking that this was more like a kind of joke, so I didn't have much reaction to it except for the confusion. But after it began to sink in, it was a bitter experience.

TG: Did you quickly decide that you would not stand for this?

JP: No, it really took me a while to figure out what I needed to do. Out of a sense of not believing that kind of harsh sentence I went back to the censors and gave them a script I had written about war, which I thought would be of interest to them. I was waiting for about a month for them to respond to me about whether they would approve that script or not but there was no response.

I had been hoping that the appeals court would reverse my ban but when I didn't hear anything about my script I began to think things were more serious. At the same time my lawyer kept telling me that this kind of sentence didn't make any sense and there was no precedent for it so I shouldn't worry.

But after a month of not hearing anything back from them I realized that the situation was more serious than I had thought. I should add that when I was arrested along with another colleague[1] we both wrote letters to the government to try to clarify our situation. My colleague's letter was accepted, and his sentence was reduced but mine was not.

TG: What kind of help do you receive from friends inside Iran?

JP: It's hard to expect other people to help you in a situation like this, especially inside Iran, because it may cause trouble for them as well. That's why I don't get in touch with a lot of people who I know because I know my telephone is being tapped. So, I really don't expect anyone in the country to do anything for me. For the same reason that I don't want to involve anyone else in my troubles, whenever I come up with an idea to do something it ends up being a very limited idea, which can be done in a very confined space with a minimum number of cast and crew.

When I made *This Is Not a Film* that caused some difficulties for my colleague Mojtaba Mirtahmasb, who was the co-director on that film and had his passport confiscated. Again, when I collaborated with Kambuzia Partovi and the actress Maryam Moqadam on *Closed Curtain* their passports were confiscated.

That's why I really have to reconsider what I'm doing and come up with a small-scale project that I can shoot and sound-record myself without involving other people. I'm even thinking about not using any actors or actresses. By necessity my movies are becoming more and more minimalistic. I realize that they will test the patience of audiences because these are not the kind of movies that I used to make or are expected of me. But in the absence of my freedom as a filmmaker that's all I can do.

TG: Why did you use co-directors on *This Is Not a Film* and *Closed Curtain*?

JP: In the case of *This Is Not a Film*, Mr. Mirtahmasb is an experienced documentary maker whereas I didn't have any experience in that kind of movie . . . [Kambuzia] Partovi, who worked on *Closed Curtain*, is a well-established screenwriter and director. I thought their experience would be valuable to me. Maybe the fact that these two filmmakers volunteered to actually work with me was their way of saying: "You're not alone in this. We're with you, we share your sentence and we share your predicament." In a sense that was their message to me and I think they sacrificed their own situations to do something for me.

TG: What was your inspiration for *Closed Curtain*?

JP: Before I made the movie, I was feeling very depressed and that's why I went to my beach house at the Caspian Sea. When I arrived, I noticed that the windows were broken so I started fixing them and made some other changes in the house.

I gradually felt my beach house could be a nice location for a movie. That's how I began to work with Mr. Partovi on writing the film's script. The important thing is that when I started working I wasn't feeling depressed any more. But at the same time, I wanted to reflect that state of mind in the movie as well so that's why it is inhabited by a kind of melancholy. The psychological touches that you see here and there in the film reflect my state of mind right before I made it.

TG: How does *Closed Curtain* differ from your previous movies?
JP: I think of myself as a realist filmmaker whose function is to reflect the surrounding environment in his movies. In my past movies I had a tendency to film a lot of exterior scenes because I had the freedom to shoot outside. But now that the authorities have forced me to abandon that environment and instead be reduced to the confines of a house, naturally my type of filmmaking has altered as well.

TG: Where did you find the wonderful dog which features so prominently in the movie?
JP: We were looking for a dog in some very different places. Finally, we ended up buying one from a peddler at a market near the Tehran cemetery where they also sell birds. I asked the vendor if it was legal to sell and buy dogs there and he replied that it was but only in that corner of the city. At first what interested us about that dog was his physique and size. But then we realized as we started playing with the dog that he was very well-trained. We left the dog with Mr. Partovi at his house so that they could get accustomed to each other. Throughout we were amazed by the kind of skills the dog kept on exhibiting.

TG: What kind of freedom of movement do you have at the moment?
JP: I don't have any limitations of movement within Iran, but I can't leave the country.

TG: What are the biggest obstacles you face as a filmmaker working on location in Iran today?
JP: It's not just me, but anybody who wants to use public locations in Iran for making a movie has to have permission from the government. Every filmmaker has to secure a government-issued permit to be able to shoot anywhere in the country. Otherwise he or she will be arrested by the police and their equipment confiscated.

So, it's a high risk to run if we work without that permit in public places. But there are ways that some filmmakers get around it. For example, they get a permit or approval to do a short film and instead they make a feature film surreptitiously.

TG: Did you have any intrusions from the authorities while you were making *This Is Not a Film* or *Closed Curtain*?

JP: We couldn't have been more careful when we were making those two movies. We confined ourselves to a house environment so basically we were only shooting interiors. Also, whenever we were discussing these projects on the phone we were quite careful not to give anything away. We were speaking a language of codes. In *Closed Curtain* when you see the black drapes inside the house we didn't use them because the movie was calling for it aesthetically but to cover up what we were doing inside the house so that nobody from outside could see us.

TG: How long did it take to shoot *Closed Curtain* and how much did it cost to make?

JP: It took us twenty-six days to shoot the film. It was a very low-budget movie because nobody received any salaries for their contributions to the film, so I ended up paying for it out of my own pocket.

TG: You have described the situation in your homeland as "the dark ages for film-making in Iran" yet there have never been so many talented Iranian filmmakers. How do you explain this?

JP: I don't see any contradiction in that in terms of how difficult the situation is for filmmaking. But at the same time, we have a lot of filmmakers, especially young talents, who have burst onto the scene and have very fresh ideas. They have emerged from the same circumstances and without trying to justify the censorship I must say that sometimes it's the restrictions that provoke the filmmakers to come up with creative solutions.

TG: *This Is Not a Film* was smuggled to the Cannes Film Festival in a flash drive hidden inside a cake. How did you get *Closed Curtain* to the Berlin Film Festival?

JP: Well, thanks to advancements in technology it's not very difficult to send a movie to a festival. All you need is to find a traveler, somebody who is going abroad, and give them your movie in a USB flash drive. This is very different from the way it used to be.

I remember when I was smuggling out my movie *The Circle* (2000) to the Venice Film Festival, I had a lot of difficulties and finally we ended up tricking the government by putting the reels of my film in a package that had the name of another movie on it. They thought they were sending a different movie to Venice.

Another time, again with *The Circle*, I had to hide the film reels in different packages and put them in different places. But all you need now is a small external hard drive to keep your movie safe somewhere.

The government used to use technology against filmmakers because in Iran if you want to make a movie you have to rent equipment from the government. This monopoly was another way they could control filmmaking but today technology is so advanced that all you need to make your movie is a small [high-definition] camera. You don't need to go to the government for equipment any more.

TG: Iranian directors like Abbas Kiarostami and Asghar Farhadi have recently been pursuing their careers abroad. Would you consider this?
JP: The idea of making a movie outside of Iran is not a bad idea and appeals to me as well. In fact, when my passport was first confiscated in Tehran Airport I was about to leave the country for Paris to negotiate with producers about making a movie outside of Iran. This was six months before I was sent to jail.[2]

So I have no problem making a movie outside, but I would like to be able to come back to Iran. I would have a very hard time if I realized that I have to stay in exile and do not have the ability to come back to my own country.

Interestingly, when I was sentenced to this ban and to imprisonment, some friends told me that maybe it was the government's way of telling me to get out of the country. It's not difficult for filmmakers to leave the country, but I don't want to flee my own country. If there is a situation whereby I can leave the country and make a movie, I would welcome that, but I need to know that I have the ability to come back.

Notes

1. Independent Iranian filmmaker Mohammad Rasoulof.
2. In the spring of 2010, Mr. Panahi spent more than three months in Tehran's Evin Prison for charges that weren't specified.

"In Prison, I Had Some Peace of Mind": Jafar Panahi on *Closed Curtain*

Vadim Rizov / 2014

From *Filmmaker* magazine, July 9, 2014. Reprinted by permission from the author.

Dogs have been banned as pets in Iran, providing the starting premise for Jafar Panahi's *Closed Curtain*. A screenwriter (Kambuzia Partovi, also the co-director) has a dog smuggled into his seaside villa by friends. Once the animal's inside, the man systematically draws the curtains over windows on all three floors. The opening of Jafar Panahi's *Closed Curtain* fictionalizes the necessary circumstances of its production: working in secret, the director was forced to draw the curtains for as much of the shoot as possible to make sure no one could see what was going on inside. There are echoes of recent scenes in Tsai Ming-liang's *Face* and Ursula Maier's *Home*—both films whose subjects methodically use tape to black out windows, an action meant to seal out a presumably threatening world. Here, the self-imposed isolation has a different intent: in order for an indoor theater to flourish, curtains reluctantly have to be drawn to keep the outside world outside, and the audience (along with the camera, which can't go beyond the porch) is trapped in the theater along with the players.

The screenwriter is trying to keep the dog's presence secret from the police, an inexact parallel with Panahi's production. The animal (named "Boy") sits and watches TV, which pours out images of bloody dying dogs assaulted by the police. Does Boy understand what he's seeing or comprehend the greater threats to his existence? Humans can know they're restricted, while the dog remains innocently oblivious; consciousness, in this context, is a curse. Already on edge, the screenwriter's equilibrium is further disrupted by the unexplained arrival of Melika (Marayam Moqadam) and Reza (Hadi Saeedi), a sister and brother seeking shelter from the police. Reza departs, but his sibling remains, annoying the screenwriter, who claims he just doesn't "want any trouble" (this in the middle of a completely illegal production, one of many meta-tricky ironies). Melika's a stubborn reminder of another type of prisoner: Iranian women, whose actions, conduct, public and private presence are all heavily regulated by the government, which is the subject of Panahi's *The Circle* and *Offside*. (The screenwriter gets to leave the house at film's end, but the woman remains locked inside; enough said.)

Panahi himself arrives later, though his relationship to the screenwriter is unclear: is the latter a product of the former's imagination? Are they aware of their side-by-side presences? Who's the specter and what's real? *Closed Curtain* repeatedly worries and rearranges these relationships and ambiguities. It's both dazzling and suffocating: as it becomes clear that what's going on could be infinitely/indefinitely tweaked, it's hard not to want Panahi to wrap it up and settle on a takeaway.

For all its frustrations, *Closed Curtain* is still a new film from one of the world's great directors, still under house arrest and forbidden from making movies. As in *The Circle* and *Crimson Gold*, the film is neatly bookended, opening and closing with a variation of the same shot, and the overall structure so intricate it's nearly palindromic. Once Panahi was an urbanist, doing for Tehran's streets roughly what Don Siegel did for San Francisco in *Dirty Harry*: shooting from afar or up close, soaking in the metropolitan bustle, making for lively and absorbing images counterbalancing grim subject matter. Now he's trapped inside, and the suffocation and lack of options is palpable in the increasingly nervous film. A gallery of posters, including ones for his past movies, are concealed under drapes: when those are pulled down, the largely non-Iranian lettering remind us this isn't the first time Panahi's work has been banned at home and easier to see abroad.

I tried to stay bloodless and focused on the art, to the extent that it can be divorced from the circumstances surrounding it, and I failed. A question about whether Panahi likes the properties of his current digital practices led back to frustration over his life, which is understandable. That Panahi's conducting standard-duty promotional activities for an illegal film while under house arrest is kind of incredible in and of itself. His interviews should be read in bulk (especially *this one* [on the *Filmmaker Magazine* website, this is a hyperlink to "Iranian Director Flouts Ban on Filmmaking" by Tobias Grey, which appears in this collection]), as part of one long update about how Panahi's doing.

Vadim Rizov: Before we talk about your new film, I'd like to ask about the DVD collection that can be seen in *This is Not a Film*, which includes a lot of new Hollywood movies I wouldn't expect you to seek out. Are these sent to you?

Jafar Panahi: Most of these are smuggled into the country and brought to people's houses through some people whose job is to distribute these illegal DVDs. Sometimes they bring my own movies to my house to buy copies from them. I should add that every major Hollywood movie is downloaded by people.

VR: How did you conceive the tricky structure?

JP: What you see in my movie is born of the circumstances that I live under, and also reflects how unsettled my frame of mind is. When I was writing the script, I wasn't feeling good at all. I was quite depressed, and that's why I went to the villa on the sea coast. When I was there, I was feeling better, but it was still in the back of my mind. I had difficulty sometimes distinguishing between what was real and what was not, and that seeped into the movie. I sometimes feel I'm still under the same circumstances. It's difficult not to have any notion of what your future is going to look like.

In prison, I had some peace of mind because I couldn't do anything. I was limited to the confines of the prison, but when you're out and you're not allowed to work, it's like you're in a larger prison. Different conditions and situations, but you still feel that you're imprisoned because of your inability to work. For a long time, I was part of society and could make socially committed and realistic movies, but now I feel isolated and can't work the way I used to work. So, I resorted to my imagination and whatever happened, it just happens in my imagination. I find it difficult to film anything that I think of, because I'm not allowed to make movies.

This is the world that they have created for me. I feel sometimes I'm the prisoner of my own thoughts. It's difficult to live in this large prison. It's like a hell in which everything seems to be internalized. I'm being forced to internalize everything, and nothing can really manifest itself the way it used to.

VR: In your earlier work, there were a lot of street scenes filmed from a distance, with lots of depth and urban hustle. How did you plan your shots when adapting to shooting in a house without those options?

JP: Working outside is what I was used to. When you go inside, you feel so limited. In our case, we couldn't even look out the window because of security. We had to pull the curtains over the window so nobody could see what we were doing inside. This is a space without a lot of depth, unlike the spaces I was using in my previous movies, and therefore the emphasis is on people rather than locations. People seem to have a larger share of the narrative. Working inside also affects the way you light any given scene, because of the closing down of the diaphragm and working with a shorter focus, which is again quite different from the way I used to work. In my previous films, if you noticed, I don't even have a shot reflecting somebody's imagination, nothing that was less than realistic. When you get to a situation like I was forced to in my last two movies, you have to follow different rules. If I had my choice, I'd love to work with exteriors and even outside of the country, as there were negotiations for that going on when I was arrested. I'd been approached to make an adaptation of Khaled Hosseini's *A Thousand Splendid Suns*.

VR: How did you conceive the part of a screenwriter who shelters "impure dogs"? It parallels your case, but not exactly.

JP: Keeping dogs as pets is illegal in Iran, especially walking them on the streets or having them ride in your car. The police can arrest you for doing something like that. People are resisting this law because they think it's unjust and they're resisting it. A lot of people keep dogs in their homes. There's even a place in Tehran where people gather and sell and buy dogs, which is quite illegal, but people still do it. There have been a lot of instances where the police show violence in grabbing dogs, even killing them in front of their owners.

VR: What do the posters on the wall signify for you when thinking about your past body of work?

JP: Most of those posters are for my own movies, but I saw the majority of the rest of them when I was a student. Obviously they affected me, but the one movie that affected me more than any other film was *The Bicycle Thieves* by Vittorio De Sica.

VR: Have you had any new contact with the government regarding your ability to make films legally again?

JP: No, unfortunately nothing new. Of course, I've never contacted the government people, but several of my friends have attempted to contact them and see if they can bring this matter to some kind of resolution. That was without my knowledge. I didn't ask them to intervene, they did it on their own. Later, they told me that they couldn't get anywhere. Unfortunately, though there may be some new people in the offices, it's the same old methods. They're showing a lot of resistance not just to me, but a lot of other filmmakers they may not like, including most recently a documentary filmmaker, Mahnaz Mohammadi.

If *Taxi Tehran* Could Have Been Presented in Iran, I Would Have Withdrawn the Film from the Official Competition at the Berlin Film Festival

Iranian Labour News Agency / 2015

From *ILNA*, February 15, 2015. Translated by Iante Roach.

Last night Iranian filmmaker Jafar Panahi won the Golden Bear at the Berlin Film Festival (25 Bahman 1393/February 14, 2015). However, he believes that had the film been presented in Iran, he would have withdrawn it from the Berlin Film Festival's official competition. We had the following brief conversation with Jafar Panahi on the occasion.

ILNA: Mr. Panahi, many congratulations on winning the Golden Bear. What are your thoughts about the prize?
Jafar Panahi: Naturally, I am very happy, both personally and for Iranian cinema.

ILNA: Have you read Mr. Ayoubi's[1] letter to the director of the Berlin Film Festival?
JP: Yes, I read it as soon as it was published.

ILNA: What did you think about it?
JP: It seemed like a polite letter to me.

ILNA: Did you have any other thoughts about it?
JP: Well, when I read it, I even asked myself, "Is that it?!" because it contained a lot of nice words, but they were merely *words*. Their value would have become clear had their speaker acted according to them.

ILNA: But Mr. Ayoubi accused the director of the Berlin Film Festival of politically tainted work. What does this have to do with Mr. Ayoubi's behavior?

JP: That's exactly where the problem begins. In our own country, we have been experiencing political interferences within the arts and especially within cinema for many years. They try to poison art with politics. Yet Mr. Ayoubi encourages others to separate art from politics! This makes us question why he does not act this way himself. And why he allows the establishment of a political barrier within the field of cinema that is longer than the Great Wall of China and taller than Milad Tower.[2]

Do you remember all the films that have been sacrificed due to this political barrier and have never been presented in cinemas, with all their creators' energy and efforts denied in the trail of the film's obstruction? In the last sentence of his letter, Mr. Ayoubi said that culture and cinema represent the eradication of fences and barriers. This sentence is beautiful in writing, but it can become eternal if put into practice. So, I believe that Mr. Ayoubi must in the first place bring down the barriers that he and his predecessors have created, and only then warn others not to build barriers.

ILNA: Considering the pressures that cinema institutions are under, what has Mr. Ayoubi not done so far and what must he do?

JP: Unfortunately, there always existed the excuse of external pressure, and there always will. Those in power have always accused us of making festival films attractive to foreign audiences, but they have hidden behind the barrier of politics and have not said openly that they never allowed us to show our films in Iran! Had this happened, the fear of Iranian films being seen in festivals abroad would have disappeared and would have been transformed into a good instrument for introducing Iranian cinema to wider audiences. For instance, this occasion would have been the best opportunity for Mr. Ayoubi to show that he does not intend to create a larger barrier. He could have used *Taxi Tehran* as an excuse for writing such a letter.

After Mr. Ayoubi's letter was published, I proposed that *Taxi Tehran* be presented during the remaining days of the Fajr Film Festival. In exchange, as an Iranian filmmaker, I would have shown my goodwill by writing a letter to the Berlin Film Festival asking for my film to be withdrawn from the official competition. Because I believe that no prize is more valuable than my own film being seen by my fellow people inside Iran.

ILNA: Do you mean that if your film had been presented at Fajr Film Festival, you would have withdrawn it from the official competition of the Berlin Film Festival?

JP: Yes, all Iranian filmmakers truly want to present their films first at home, but the political barrier has always prevented certain films from being screened in Iran.

ILNA: Is that all?
JP: Yes, that's all! Even though I never send messages to authorities, I made this proposition to Mr. Ayoubi through another filmmaker just five minutes after his letter was published.

ILNA: And what was his reaction?
JP: He sent me a message saying that he would discuss the matter with his advisers. I waited for his decision up until the last day of Fajr Film Festival. If you want to double-check, you can follow up with Mr. Ayoubi.

Notes

1. Hojatollah Ayoubi was then head of Iran's Cinema Organization, operating under the auspices of the Ministry of Culture and Islamic Guidance.
2. This is the sixth-tallest tower in the world, standing 435 meters tall in downtown Tehran.

This Is Not an Interview

Ehsan Khoshbakht and Drew Todd / 2018

May 11, 2018. The translator wishes to remain anonymous.

Editor's preface: This interview was conducted by telephone a few days before Panahi's latest film, *3 Faces*, premiered at Cannes Film Festival, where it won a best screenplay prize. Drew Todd's questions were sent to me in advance so I could translate them for Panahi. However, the Iranian director preferred the conversation to be more spontaneous, thus some improvisation was necessary.—EK

Drew Todd: It is often reported that you are under "house arrest"...

Jafar Panahi: I am not under house arrest. I can leave my house and go anywhere within the borders of Iran, but I am prohibited from leaving the country.

Ehsan Khoshbakht: Obviously there are a lot of misconceptions surrounding you and your current situation; how important do you feel it is to correct those misconceptions?

JP: The thing is—I can't understand how anyone can even bring up the term "house arrest" when I am still making and releasing new films. I went to the north of Iran and shot *Closed Curtain* by the Caspian Sea. I made *Taxi* on the streets of Tehran. How else can I prove that I am not under house arrest? Why does this false information keep being repeated? I don't know.

EK: When I try to explain this to my non-Iranian colleagues, they suspect that I might have something against you—that perhaps I had an ulterior motive for trying to assert that you were not under house arrest.

JP: I am banned from leaving the country. My sentence totals eighty-six years. I've been handed four twenty-year bans: a travel ban, a ban on writing scripts, a ban on directing films, and a ban on giving interviews; and also six years imprisonment. I am simply banned from leaving the country.

EK: Among the litany of false information concerning you, some sources also report that your prison sentence has been revoked. I keep telling people that your prison sentence has not been revoked in any way whatsoever.

JP: None of my sentences has been revoked. The authorities could show up at any moment to enforce them.

EK: What is it like, trying to make films under these circumstances? How does it affect you, knowing that these penalties could be enforced at any time?

JP: I don't think about it at all. I will cross that bridge when I come to it. I am a filmmaker and all I can do for now is continue making films.

DT: Since you were banned from making films for a period of twenty years, which of course has not actually stopped you from making them, your life and your films have been visibly intertwined. But I wonder if you think they've always been, from day one?

JP: That is exactly what it means to be a filmmaker who focuses on society and social issues—we look at conditions within our society and take inspiration from them when making our films. But I am not allowed to draw inspiration from society anymore; I am not a part of society. That obviously affects me and is something that I reflect on. My personal experiences now play a much greater role in my work than society does. In other words, my inspiration comes from my own present circumstances and is then transferred into society, rather than being the other way around. It is almost as if an entire society exists within me.

DT: Resistance/defiance is a running theme throughout your life and films. Did coming of age as a filmmaker during the revolution and its backlash against cinema inform this theme of defiance? Where else might this come from, do you think?

JP: No. No, that has nothing to do with it. I am a filmmaker and ultimately I just want to make films. I will always find a way to make them. I only understand film and cinema; there are no other influences. I only look for different ways to make my films. I don't know if you would call that "defiance" or something else. It is called "filmmaking." Filmmakers make films; they cannot do anything other than that. As a filmmaker I am simply exploring every possible avenue to assist in the filmmaking process.

DT: I imagine some might be surprised to see Luis Buñuel on your list of influences and inspirations. Yet when I think of Buñuel, I think of how his movies—whether produced in Spain or France or Mexico—shine a light on the fault lines particular to the society and era surrounding him. Could you talk about how a surrealist critique of power structures informs your own cinematic critiques of social structures?

JP: That is the purpose of social commentary in film, regardless of what approach is taken, whether surrealist or something else. When a filmmaker observes something unfair and unjust in society, it is reflected in his reaction to those social conditions. Through that reaction, his film begins to take shape. This creative process, this early stage in the development of a film, can be applied to surrealism, cinematic realism, Iranian neorealism, and other movements in cinema.

DT: In a related sense, many of your films bridge this theoretical divide between realism, on the one hand, and modernism, on the other. This is to say, your cinema is not just neorealist, as many claim on first impression, but also experimental, absurdist, and self-reflexive. How do you feel you reconcile this, and to what end?

JP: I myself don't really know. The way in which my films are analyzed and their symbolism is deconstructed is based on the interpretations of film critics. It has nothing to do with me.

DT: Regardless of your films' genre or mood, you have a knack for ending your films cathartically and poignantly but also without a complete sense of finality. As a storyteller and filmmaker, what do you want to leave your audiences with at the end of your films? What do you strive for in your finales?

JP: Whenever I start to write or develop a new film, the first things that I think about are the beginning and the ending of the film. I believe that the beginning of every film must be strong enough to hold the audience's attention for the first fifteen minutes and compel them to continue watching. The film must firmly establish itself during those first fifteen minutes; otherwise, the audience will lose interest. The end of the film must also be powerful enough to leave a lasting impression on its audience. If the ending is weak, then the audience will simply forget about the film. Whereas if the beginning and the ending are both strong, then the audience will continue to think about the film even after leaving the movie theatre; it will stay in the minds of audience members and they will reflect on it subconsciously. If the end of the film is weak or unmemorable, however, it will quickly be forgotten.

DT: Speaking of endings, my students always ask, "What was the alternate ending of *Offside*, in the case Iran had lost to Bahrain?!"

JP: I really don't know! We had only written about half of the screenplay, and the rest was left unfinished. We shot the film around the time of the actual match, so we would have had to change the story depending on the result and what happened.

DT: Could you tell us something about a few films you've started and didn't get to finish, films such as *Pol* (*Bridge*), *Bazgasht* (*Return*), and the film you were working on when you were arrested and imprisoned.

JP: *Pol* was the first film that I ever worked on. I remember that I had just watched all of Alfred Hitchcock's films around that time and, influenced by him, I had everything about my film planned to the finest detail. I had storyboards drawn for every shot, actors and actresses for every character, cameramen and film crew; I had everything organized—everything planned in advance. I went to work with a very clear vision and I did everything according to my plan. When it came to post-production and editing, there was absolutely nothing wrong with the film in terms of structure and basic cinematic conventions—everything was fine. But I felt that the film lacked soul. I mean, everything about the film was done right but it all just felt a little fake; it had lost its sense of realism. Even though I was not well-known at the time and no one really knew or understood what I was capable of as a director, I simply felt that the film could not be part of my filmography. That's why I stole the reels from the archive and destroyed them. That was the story of *Pol*.

We spent four or five years trying to produce *Bazgasht*, which at the time was just a screenplay, because I thought that I wanted to make a war film. Iran was at war during that time and, whether I liked it or not, I had convinced myself that I had to support my country through the medium of film. After the war ended, a number of films emerged that attempted to justify the war in some way or another, but ultimately the war genre has always been about humans and humanity. That is precisely what *Bazgasht* was: a compassionate film set during the end of the war, after the UN resolution was passed and troops began to withdraw from the front lines. Unfortunately, despite all the effort that I put into the film, they did not allow me to do it; they kept questioning why I would want to make a war film. Despite the fact that the censor had read the screenplay, they suspected that I intended to do something else with the film.

Then there was the film that I began working on with Mohammad Rasoulof, which took place during the post-June 2009 election and centered on a family. The film was about thirty percent complete when they stopped us from making it.

EK: You mentioned Alfred Hitchcock in relation to your first film—although your films are very different, certain techniques associated with directors of other eras and styles can be found in your work, such as your masterful use of long takes as in *Rope* and *Under Capricorn*.

JP: During my time as a student, I had a professor, Mr. Zabeti Jahromi, who was an expert on Soviet cinema and Sergei Eisenstein. His main interest was in breaking down the scene into small shots. One day I asked him how long a shot should last, and he told me that it should cut away as soon as it has said all that it needs to say. *Pol* was a film that said everything it needed to say but lacked an extra ingredient that I couldn't quite put my finger on at the time. When a shot lingers, the film is notifying the audience that they are being told everything they need to know and at that moment they should focus on whatever feelings are being conveyed. Just like in the opening paragraph of *Chronicle of a Death Foretold*, when Gabriel García Márquez writes that Santiago Nasar got up at five-thirty in the morning on the day that he was killed—the reader is given one small piece of information and that is all. Of course, the book goes on to gradually explain how the event unfolded.

EK: I was at the premiere of *Taxi* in Berlin and I was completely surprised by the hostile response it got from Iranian critics. Why do you think they, or at least a large number of them, are reacting to your latest works with such hostility?

JP: I really don't concern myself with what critics might say; that's not what I think about when I make a film. With every film I have produced over the past four years, I have always maintained the belief that it is crucial for me to continue making films in any way possible. In other words, the mere act of filmmaking is more important to me than anything else. Those sentences were passed to prevent me from making any more films, so I knew I had no choice but to continue making them.

Government propaganda in Iran is unfortunately so widespread and overpowering that even when the most open-minded among us actually enjoy something, for example when they start to praise one of my films, some small piece of propaganda seated in the back of their mind will make them say, "This is certainly a good film, but . . ." If one of my films receives an award, for example, they assume it must be for political reasons or something else. Whatever the government says about me always manages to find its way into popular opinion sooner or later, and it just goes to show how much of an influence my situation has and how impressionable they are. Of course there are some critics who are able to decide whether my films are good or bad based on their own valid reasons, without being hateful or influenced by disinformation.

EK: Your latest films are road movies of a sort, and of course you knew Abbas Kiarostami very well. How much of an influence did your experience as his assistant have on you, and what did your friendship with Kiarostami mean to you?

JP: When I had those formative experiences; I was first learning about the fundamentals of filmmaking and the films of Alfred Hitchcock, and tried to adapt and apply those lessons. Then I met Kiarostami who wrote somewhere about me that when he worked with me, he was able to appreciate the luxury of having a good assistant for the first time. We had the same ideas and inclinations because we shared the same approach to filmmaking. There were times when I understood exactly what he wanted and I had everything prepared before he could even say a word. But *Crimson Gold,* which was written by Kiarostami, doesn't resemble a Kiarostami film and takes a different path. That's where our views differ. But at the end of the day, we were both noncommercial, humanist filmmakers. He was more interested in the poetic side of that humanist cinema and I was more interested in the social side of it.

Index

CPSIA information can be obtained
at www.ICGtesting.com
Printed in the USA
BVHW030439260419
546487BV00003B/4/P